To [handwritten] end +
members of our
very

FAST LANE
TO FAITH

special [handwritten]
TWA [handwritten]

A JET JOCKEY'S SEARCH
FOR SIGNIFICANCE

family [handwritten]

your friend [handwritten]

BERT BOTTA

Bert [handwritten]

415 320 9811 [handwritten]

ENGAGE
FAITH
PRESS

Published 2013 by Engage Faith Press

Printed in the United States of America

17 16 15 14 13   1 2 3 4

ISBN: 978-1-936672-43-1

Library of Congress Control Number: 2012954318

FAST LANE TO FAITH

I dedicate my book to the most important women in my life, my mother, Marie, and my wife, Janeth.

Mom believed in me when I didn't know how to believe in myself.

My wife, Janeth, took up the cross where my mother left off. She has the power of a no-nonsense, mature woman combined with the alluring innocence of a little girl, wrapped in a four-foot-eleven, ninety-nine-pound package of Latina TNT.

Oftentimes when I go about pitying myself, I fail to realize I'm being blown across the sky on great winds.

—Ojibway saying

CONTENTS

ACKNOWLEDGMENTS

Regardless of what I wrote in my book about my father, I thank him for providing me with the "fuel for the fire" that burns in my belly for the work I've done on myself and with other men.

He passed on to me the energy, the passion, the strength, and the courage that I have found in myself. He did the best he could with the legacy of old-country Italy that he inherited. Thanks, Pop. I only wish you could have stuck around long enough to be on a New Warrior weekend with me.

I thank my mom for her steadfast, enduring, deep faith in God that she infused into everything she did. Her quiet, unassuming strength and belief in God was an example for me long before I knew I needed that.

I often think of the nuns, priests, and brothers who taught me and who saw something in me that took years for me to discover. To name but a few of the many: Father Casey, Father Joe Priestley, Father Geary, Father Hayburn, and the ladies in black from my former Catholic grammar school, St. Paul's in the Mission district of San Francisco: Sister Mary Johanna, Sister Mary Artura, and Sister Mary Francine.

Thank you, Uncle Pete, for being the man in my life who first demonstrated to me the power of an older man caring for and passing on his knowledge to a younger one. Thanks, Pete, for also instilling in me a love for things mechanical. I'm glad I took it upon myself to see you in Klamath Falls just before you went home to the Lord.

To my brothers of the New Warrior network whom I trained under, staffed with, worked alongside, and prepped food with: Thank you for loving, supporting, and challenging me into becoming the man I am today.

To my Living From the Heart Christian brothers, who now form the nucleus of our Wednesday-night group: The bonds we have formed are among the strongest I have experienced in twenty-five years of doing men's work. I'm sure that's because we acknowledge the power of God in our lives. We also carry that acknowledgement into our work together, in a way that constitutes worship like we've never known worship before.

And most importantly, I thank my beautiful, intelligent, wise, no-nonsense, and faithful wife, Janeth. She has blessed my life beyond anything I could have imagined in a way that only God could have arranged.

INTRODUCTION

What you are about to read is the result of overcoming years of procrastination, fear, and the ongoing conquest of not feeling good enough.

I picked the theme for my book, or should I say, it picked me, because my feeling of not being good enough is part of why I've felt insignificant for most of my life. When I don't feel significant, I feel afraid—that I won't be smart enough, that I won't be loved, that I'm not able to love, that I can't make decisions on my own, ad nauseam.

This fear has ruled much of my life. It has led to the loss of large sums of money by my not trusting my own ability to make intelligent choices, or by not doing my own due diligence before throwing money at investments. It has led to the loss of important relationships; the fear of entering into relationships with the kind of women I would have loved to be with but was afraid to approach; buying motorcycles on a fixed, declining retirement income; and more.

Despite this, I have been successful in more than one venture. I recently finished a flying career that rewarded me with the opportunity to travel to most countries in the world, to find and court my wife in Colombia, and to develop a love for the people in the aviation industry, who are truly a unique family.

I also had a successful career as a licensed counselor, certified leader of men, personal life coach, and writer.

But my life could have taken more beneficial turns had I become aware of my emotional "wounds" earlier.

Too many men die way before their time because of the impact that emotional wounds exact on their physical and emotional health.

Our ability to give and, more importantly, to receive love has been shortchanged by an absence of strong, supportive, loving men in our lives whom we could trust and model ourselves after.

It has only been over the last twenty years that I now realize the importance of having men in my life whom I can be honest with, whom I can trust, who will support me when I'm down and when I'm up, who are capable of seeing my gifts and my emotional wounds, and who will hold me accountable for my actions while continuing to love me and not abandon me when things get rough. This might be a novel idea to some of you, as this kind of intimacy is rare—but attainable—in our society.

We need to (1) Take the time to feel our hearts and recognize their cries for intimacy and the need to connect with others; (2) Acknowledge the fear in doing so; (3) Make a committed, sincere effort to break through that fear; and (4) Take action to include ourselves in activities that attract us.

My desire for wanting to share my story with other men and women grew out of one of the most important and powerful events of my life: a weekend training, in August 1992, called the New Warrior Training Adventure, an adult men's rite of passage.

Rites of passage were a core part of the ancient tribal community, where young boys at the age of puberty were taken from the safety of their villages and "initiated" into manhood by male extended-family members and other trusted elders who were models of safety, strength, wisdom, and maturity in their tribes.

We modern-day men have lost the connection to this ancient, powerful ritual.

That weekend changed my life. On a dirty, old (yet sacred) carpet in the middle of a great room in a weather-beaten, rustic lodge in the middle of a forest in northern Wisconsin, the men surrounding me helped me to purge years of pent-up anger, rage, shame, and the emotional poison of feeling like I never measured up to just about every man to whom I compared myself.

Something magical happened that weekend; waves of joy washed over me as I literally leapt up and ran around the room after I was able to release the venom from within me. My heart felt as light as a feather as I unabashedly hugged other men and told them of the love that now gushed out of my heart for them.

These things are impossible to measure unless I look in the rearview mirror of my life and compare what I see from my past to what my life looks like now.

Up until that weekend, I had never been shown—by strong, loving, supportive, safe men—who I was capable of becoming.

That training also opened the door to my being able to accept that I was a talented, loving, loved, and capable man.

That weekend formed the beginning stages of finding my true mission in life; it showed me the power that a newly opened heart has, and I used it to help transform my life and the lives of other men whom I would eventually work with.

Shortly after I returned from that weekend to my home at the time in St. Louis, I knew I needed this work—this connection with other men.

I looked around and saw nothing even remotely like what I had experienced in that training. There was especially nothing like the intimacy, honesty, or accountability in the churches that I visited, nothing like it in my relationships with the pilots whom I shared the same cockpits with, nothing like it in my relationships with the women in my life—especially the woman I was married to at the time.

So I started the first New Warrior men's community in St. Louis. I began to organize the same trainings that I had just attended. I started speaking in bookstores, libraries—anywhere people would listen— about the importance of this work. I explained that it wasn't just to benefit men, because acknowledging the pain that we all carry, because of our emotional wounding, has an impact on the women in our lives, on our kids, and on the survival of our planet.

As a result of returning to the Christian spiritual practice of my youth, I recently started a Christian men's group in my home county of Marin.

My faith now drives my values and my mission, which is to reach and teach men the power of uncovering, acknowledging, and transforming their lives through the use of the new clarity, energy, and healthy power that emerges from those tapped emotions.

I call the essence of my work, "Helping men to open their hearts, so God can more easily do His work."

I'm writing this book to share with you, the men who may struggle with similar problems, not only my story but also the lessons I've learned in my lifetime.

I have learned, mostly through working with over two thousand men for six years as a certified leader in the New Warrior Training Adventure, that even the most outwardly confident of men—the kind of men to whom I often compare myself—harbor secret feelings of insecurity, fear, shame, inadequacy, cowardice, and more.

My love and passion for being part of a community of men who support each other, and who have learned how to be open and honest about what they're feeling, has led me to start three men's communities and to write this book.

I want you, my readers, in my life in a way that we can support one another and speak with clarity, courage, and wisdom about all aspects of our lives: spiritual, financial, emotional, and physical.

Our lives here on earth are astonishingly short. I want and need to have you in my life in ways that are clearer to me now than ever before.

I have started groups in St. Louis, Missouri; Taos, New Mexico; and Marin County, in the North Bay region of San Francisco, California.

My book is also about my desire to pass on to men, and the women in their lives, what I have learned. I want this for you, so your learning curve can be shortened and you can get on with what you are really good at and were born to do.

For the men who are reading this, I want you to know how close you are to experiencing the joy, the excitement, the true sense of adventure that a life closely examined brings.

I want you to know that you can have a life free of the shackles of fear and self-judgment, and still be a "real man" and continue to enjoy what guys love to do.

This book can help to open the eyes of your heart; it can help you to see how immeasurably more powerful and enjoyable your life can be without unconsciously fending off the love and support of those around you.

It's risky for me to put out in print that I want and need you in my life. But to withhold this request would be to deny the connection that I need in order to grow in all aspects of my life.

I hope you feel the same way after reading my book.

CHAPTER 1
THE WAKE-UP CALL

Don't ask yourself what the world needs. Ask yourself what
makes you come alive and then go do that. Because what the
world needs is people who have come alive.

—Howard Thurman

It was 1981. I was forty-one years old, and I had been flying as a pilot for Trans World Airlines (TWA) for fourteen years. This was my dream job; I was a commercial airline pilot for one of the premier airlines of the sixties and most of the seventies.

I was making more money than I ever thought possible. I was a health nut, running 10K races and marathons, eating organic vegetables and tofu, and scrounging for wild dandelions at the local Marin County salad bars.

But something was missing; my life was not as idyllic as I thought it was. A divorce from my third wife was pending. When I first met her, Joyce, I fell head over heels in love. Or so I thought. But my idea of love would turn out to be not quite the same as hers.

My idea of love was her being willing to ride on the back of my motorcycle, accompanied by a group of my riding buddies; her attending my many running races; us being constantly on the move, traveling to India, taking motorcycle trips, camping with friends.

Her idea of love was trying to get me to make time for "sacred" activities: hanging out together with no agenda, taking walks in the woods, holding hands, touching one another without it necessarily leading to lovemaking, taking weekends off with no races planned, not answering phone calls on the first or second ring, not hanging out with the running club every weekend, not writing another article or flying off somewhere on free airline passes on my days off from my regular flying, etc.

But this was not to be my typical divorce. Joyce would be the first woman to leave me. I had been the judge and jury in my other marriages. I had been the one to make the decision to leave my other wives. Man, I was in control!

In those halcyon days of the sixties and seventies, my job as a pilot came with enough prestige and money to impress me and more than my share of the ladies. I had free, worldwide travel benefits, all the toys that any man could ever hope for, and a home in Marin County, California, one of the most affluent and beautiful places in the United States.

After Joyce left me, I figured, "Hell, I'll just take up where I left off, find another woman [like I had done with all the rest], and continue to fly airplanes and get on with my life."

My marriage to Joyce had ended after a little over three years. She didn't leave me for another man or for a career. She left me because I wasn't there for her—physically, emotionally, or spiritually.

She warned me repeatedly, months ahead of time, that she would leave unless I spent more time with her.

All my doings were distractions that I had occupied myself with to continue churning along on the hamster wheel of my life—that spinning, circular cage that I stepped into every day of my life in an unconscious grind to keep from looking at what actually made me run.

Looking back now, I was afraid of what I might feel if I stopped long enough. I might feel the pain of the unconscious behavior that drove me to enter into marriages without the slightest idea of the consequences of my actions, or I might realize the deeper commitment, beyond "let's go for a ride today," that was required to make marriage successful, or anything else for that matter.

My career as a pilot for this prestigious, world-renowned airline was so far beyond any accomplishment I could have imagined as a kid that it had become my safety net; it was my fallback position that would insulate me from any personal problem or event or even divorce, so I thought.

I could merely gather up my uniform and my navigation kit, move out and move on, and show up for the next flight—with a new crew of potential flight-attendant lovers—that would take me somewhere, anywhere.

Flying was the perfect match for my flying boy personality. One of the mythical Greek stereotypes was the flying boy, Icarus, who flew too close to the sun and melted the wax that held his man-made wings together. By his careless, carefree action, he fell to his death in the sea.

The camaraderie of my flight crews—the joy that we shared in doing something that a very small segment of the population was privileged to do, and the bonding that took place when we flew around the world on a ten-day trip together—insulated me from the world that existed outside my airline shell.

My flying career was my safety net, my identity. Outside the cockpit, I needed to make sure I totally identified with my pilot image if anyone asked me what I did.

I was so enamored with my role as a pilot, and especially with my idolization of military pilots, that whenever anyone asked me if I flew in the military, I would answer, yes. I hoped they wouldn't ask me specifically what kind of aircraft I flew, or what squadron I was in, or when I was in flight school.

Since I had been an enlisted, nonpilot crewmember in the navy, I knew the aviation jargon and whatever other flight credibility pieces I needed to maintain this façade.

But most importantly, I was allowed to work with my heroes, the naval aviators whom I especially idolized. When I enlisted in the navy, I had wanted to fly. But as a seventeen-year-old enlisted kid, I didn't think I was smart enough to make it through flight school, and especially not smart enough to make it on and off "the boat," the aircraft carrier that all naval aviators are required to qualify to land on.

So I projected my hopes and dreams of flight onto these men who had been so influential in shaping my flying career through my close association with them as a crewmember on their aircraft. They became my heroes. The funny thing is, to this day, they still are.

What I didn't realize, with Joyce and the other women in my life, was that I was dependent on having a woman in my life, not as a companion but more as an emotional talisman.

They were good-luck charms who bore some kind of psychological and emotional security for me. I could always return to them if I needed the kind of emotional support that I couldn't feel for myself.

After gaining cursory comfort from them, I'd continue my romp through life, inevitably returning to my woman *de jour* when I needed my emotional batteries recharged.

It wouldn't be until years later that I would feel the pain, the shame, and the remorse of my insensitivity toward the women in my life. I had hurt so many women who had placed their trust in me, who had loved me with everything they had, only for me to not be able to receive that trust and love by my selfishly keeping on "being Bert."

After many years and a few more relationship challenges, I now have a beautiful woman in my life, whom I'm extremely careful to be tender with and to treat with the kind of love, respect, and tenderness that I was unconscious of in my past relationships.

I want you to learn these lessons without you, or others, having to go through the kind of pain and torment that I went through.

FLYING WHILE IMPAIRED

Two weeks after Joyce left, I lumbered up the three flights of stairs that led to the pilot's mailroom on the second floor of TWA's big red-and-white hangar on the southwest corner of San Francisco International Airport.

This building was where the flight operations office for the San Francisco pilots' domicile (flight base) was housed.

As I climbed the stairs, I felt a weight, a heaviness, deeper than anything I had ever felt before. I knew I needed to somehow take a break from flying.

During the weeks since Joyce had left, I was missing radio calls and frequency changes from air traffic control; my usual good flying was erratic. But besides the dull ache of emotional pain, I thought I was doing pretty good.

In fact, I was a safety hazard, an emotional wreck waiting to happen.

But, being the tough guy that I was, I didn't want to admit that I couldn't hold my life together. Instead, I thought to myself, *Man, I should be able to handle this. What the hell's the matter with me?* Asking for help was the last thing on my mind.

I felt weak and helpless, and I had no place to turn. I couldn't turn to my friends and admit that I was out of control. What would they think? But I knew I needed help before I literally crashed and burned and, because of my line of work, took others with me.

I walked down the long, sanitary, whitewashed hallway in the hangar and knocked on my flight manager's door. The bottom of the door was made from a rich, darkly stained hardwood, and the top was a window with that milky, translucent glass where you can see the shapes of people moving around behind it, but you can't quite make out who they are.

I knocked on the door.

"Come on in!"

"Hey, Frank, how ya doin'? I just wanted to talk to you about somethin' I'm going through... "

With those words barely out of my mouth, I started to cry. I didn't want to, but I had no control over the tears that poured down my cheeks. The tears flooded down onto my white uniform shirt and splashed onto my dark blue uniform jacket with the beautiful, gold-embossed TWA wings pinned on the left front side.

I can still remember my thoughts: *Shit, man, you're losin' it in front of people you've known for the last fourteen years.*

I could see it right then, stamped in bold letters across the front of my next annual fitness report: "Emotionally unstable under pressure. Not recommended for captain upgrade."

I thought, *Man, they must really think you're some kinda wimp.* This was definitely not part of my plan.

EARLY SIGNS OF EVERYDAY MAGIC

I didn't know it at the time, but those tears touched the heart of my flight manager, the part of him that was still raw from his own divorce just a few short years before.

After I stopped crying, he told me, "Bert, take as much time off as you need. When you're ready to come back, just call in, and we'll put you back on schedule."

I was shocked. I was used to hiding my feelings, if I was even remotely able to determine what they were, because I thought I would be seen as weak if I expressed them.

This is what most men learn growing up under dads and other men who are out of touch with their feelings: It's a sign of weakness to show our feelings, to cry, to admit that we're wrong, and to show affection to other men, to women, to kids.

We're unconsciously living out the legacy that was passed down to us from our fathers and the other men in our lives who were emotionally deprived and wounded.

Yet here I was, being more vulnerable and transparent than I ever had been, and this "company man" was giving me as much time off as I needed to take a paid vacation and put my life back together!

This definitely did not compute in my left-brain way of perceiving the world. Up to that point, I'd always figured everything out rationally, logically, in a linear fashion. If it didn't "make sense," I didn't understand it.

This definitely didn't make sense to me. Yet, with this irrational example of my flight manager's compassion, I was learning there was another way to comprehend life. To top that, the man sitting in front of me represented company management; he was definitely not to be trusted, according to what was taught by our union's Labor/Management Relations 101.

This was the beginning of a slow but steady realization that knowing what my truth was and then living it out—being human and vulnerable, as painful and uncool as that seemed to be—would be like having a magic wand that the fairy godmother of my childhood would wave to create my own perfect world.

The men I was taught to look up to as a kid—I call them part of "The John Wayne syndrome"—were the cool guys, tough as nails, unapproachable by mere mortals, who rode off into the sunset on horseback saying, "I don't need no stinkin' love in my life; I got my horse," the "love 'em and leave 'em" symbols of manhood; these guys were my role models growing up.

How the hell else was I supposed to act? I had forty-two years of programming driving me!

CHAPTER 2
TRAINING WHEELS

I was a loner growing up, with the kinds of doubts about my abilities that plague a lot of kids. As a result, I isolated myself from others, and by doing that, learned how to cut myself off from true friendships with other men and, ultimately, many women as well.

What I didn't know at the time was that I needed to be reassured that I was okay, that I was significant, that I was loved. Pop was incapable of giving me these things because he hadn't received them from his father.

As a result of my not being heard or asked for my opinion as a kid, I now find great satisfaction in expressing myself through the written word. I discovered that when I write, I can express what is really in my heart. To this day, I often write my prayers.

My father's philosophy was the old-school "kids should be seen and not heard"; unfortunately for me, this worked really well. It squelched much of my curiosity, and it put a lid on my creativity and joy.

In a New Age conference I attended, I heard that we pick our parents for the lessons we need to learn. If this is the case, I couldn't have picked a better Pop because I have been digging my way out from underneath his "gifts": the rubble of self-judgment, unworthiness, and lack of confidence that I lived under for so many years.

My father was incapable of expressing his feelings and his love for and appreciation of me. I interpreted that lack as my not being good enough for love, for anything. That colored everything I did and everyone I came to be in a relationship with. It obviously also led to my feeling unworthy.

I eventually came to realize, after I was capable of forgiveness, that my Pop was merely reenacting what was passed on to him by his father, and his father before him, and so on down the line.

I needed and wanted recognition for who I was as a young man. I wanted the love and support of other men, in addition to the stingy kind of love I received from Pop.

But by the time I was nine years old, it was too late to get those things from Pop. I needed to have something I could call my own, something that reflected who I was as a unique kid with unlimited possibilities. That's important to a nine-year-old kid with his whole life ahead of him.

FIRST FLIGHT

My love for speed, flying, and being "above it all" grew in me throughout my life from the time I went for my first airplane ride. I was eight or nine years old when Pop took me to Half Moon Bay Airport, on the coast, just south of San Francisco, for the first time.

Pop had an interest in airplanes, though he never showed it. I guess that rubbed off on me: both the interest in planes and not showing it.

As it is with most men, I was taught to not show my emotions, my feelings; that it wasn't "cool" to be expressive with my joy or laughter. It was definitely okay to show my anger, though.

We were standing alongside one of the hangars on the northwest end of the field when a beautiful, yellow Piper J3 Cub "taildragger" taxied by us and parked. After the prop quit turning, a big man, probably six-foot-four or six-five, swung open the left-side fabric-covered fuselage door and unfolded himself out of the tiny craft.

He straightened up to his full height, looked over at me, and said, "Hey, Son, it looks like you could use a ride."

I looked up and over at Pop. He just looked away as if to say, "Whatever." He didn't say yes or no. I took that as a yes!

I walked slowly over to the Cub, and the big guy introduced himself as Bill and reached out his hand. I slowly reached my hand out, and he shook it; he had a gentle touch for such a big man.

He walked around to the passenger-side door, unlatched it, and motioned for me to climb into the front tandem seat. (With the Cub's tandem seating, the pilot flies from the back seat.) He picked me up and scrunched me into the bucket seat.

He reached in and buckled me into the seat with the big, heavy, olive-drab army-surplus seat belt.

Then he climbed into the back seat, buckled himself in, reached down, yelled, "Clear," and turned the ignition switch to "start." The propeller didn't go through more than three swings of the blade, and the little engine fired right off.

Now, you have to know that to a nine-year-old boy who wasn't feeling real great about himself, this was indescribably big stuff. I can't adequately describe the rush, the exhilaration, the light-headedness, the feeling of excitement in my stomach that I felt then and would often feel, to a lesser degree, thirty and forty years in the future.

That feeling would often overtake me when I taxied onto the runway in position for takeoff as a pilot in any of the aircraft I flew. I would again feel the almost uncontainable, indescribable feeling of exhilaration and joy that coursed through my body on that first flight in that little Piper Cub.

That ten-minute flight around "the patch," as aviators call a short flight around the airport, set the tone for my life in the air; I had found a way to move much faster over the ground than I was ever able to before.

My pop was a hard-working, second-generation Italian, who was one of the top chefs in the San Francisco restaurant business in the 1940s, '50s, and '60s.

He was also a gifted freehand caricature artist who never really did anything to express that talent. My judgment of Pop was that his frustration and fear of "putting himself out there" as an artist manifested itself inwardly. The impact on me was that our interactions were tainted with his fear and frustration.

He also didn't have men in his own life whom he could look up to, be mentored by, and use as role models for what a healthy, loving man and father should look and act like.

This led to me having to make up what I thought a young man was supposed to be and act like. And I got it wrong most of the time.

Since I couldn't get the kind of tools that I needed for my own healthy development from Pop, and since I didn't have any other men in my life whom I could turn to, I set out to literally build a vehicle that I figured would give me the significance, recognition, and power I couldn't get from the world I found myself in.

This would be something that I could pour my frustrations, anger, and resentments into. I would look back at my life later and feel sad that I missed out on dating women, missed my junior and senior proms, and missed most of the normal social activities that healthy young men engage in. Instead, I replaced social activities with hours spent in my parents' basement, pouring my heart and soul into building my "escape vehicle."

MY FIRST MENTOR

I was ten years old and had made friends with an older boy, Gene, in our neighborhood. He owned an early version of a modern-day, mini motor scooter. It was called a Doodlebug.

The first time I was able to borrow the 'Bug from Gene, I was hooked. This little beast would form a major part of my basic "escape-vehicle training."

Lucky for me, Gene had graduated to one of the early small motorcycles, a 125cc BSA Bantam, so I had pretty much unlimited access to the 'Bug.

Some other rising young hooligans and I would regularly terrorize the neighborhood and its occupants on our various motorized scooters and the many small motorcycles of the day.

After two years of riding the Doodlebug whenever I got the chance, I had honed some pretty good riding skills. But the initial thrill of riding the 'Bug began to wear off; I started to feel the need for something bigger and faster.

Whenever I would talk to Pop about my burning need for a real motor scooter—a Cushman—it seemed as if he never heard me. So, like I often did, I took his silence as an "affirmative" and moved ahead with my plans to buy my first scooter.

I badgered my parents relentlessly to let me buy a full-sized motor scooter with my paper-route money. They finally relented, but not before I laid out my "business plan" on how I could increase my newspaper route profits by using a scooter to throw more papers more easily on my early-morning route.

What I didn't tell them was that I would also be able to scoot down the sidewalks of San Francisco's Sunnyside neighborhood (an oxymoron in the fogbound, windward side of the Twin Peaks area where I lived), throwing papers on my route and free to do whatever I wanted to do.

It was September 1951. I was twelve years old, and Mom, Pop, and I were visiting the Italian side of our family—my grandfather, grandmother, aunts, and uncles on my father's side—in Fresno, California. Fresno's typical, oppressive summer heat had just started to cool.

After our first week in Fresno, I asked my Uncle Pete (who was married to Pop's sister, Auntie Anita) if he would help me find a motor scooter, make sure it was in good shape, and help me buy it.

Pete was a master mechanic and a jack-of-all-trades. He and my aunt owned a small truck body and tank repair shop in the industrial section of Fresno. Pete and I started looking at the classified ads in *The Fresno Bee*, the local newspaper.

We found a scooter for sale on the outskirts of Fresno. Pete drove us over there in his old, black Model A Ford coupe with a small trailer attached, so that if I bought the scooter, we could load it into the trailer. This Model A would be the same little car that I would take my first driving lessons in, on one of my later trips to Fresno.

The scooter was beautiful. It was an early-model Cushman with a one-and-a-half horsepower Briggs and Stratton motor and a two-speed transmission. It was bright maroon, and the tail section tapered off in the most beautiful gradual sweep of any machine I had ever seen. This was my scooter.

I had brought $75 of my hard-earned, paper-route money with me to Fresno. Pete did the negotiating, and I shelled out my $75. Pete said to me, "Junior, you ride it back to the shop, and I'll follow you instead of us loading it into the trailer."

"Are you sure, Uncle Pete?"

"Heck yes. If you're going to ride it home to San Francisco, let's make sure you can at least get it back to the shop."

That was all I needed. I rode it back to his shop, and when I pulled up in front and put the kickstand down, I just stood there for a minute or so and took in the fact that I had driven this beautiful machine, by myself, all the way across town.

As a kid, I had learned how to be a good boy; I learned how to be seen and not heard. I learned how to stay invisible, and as a result, I felt powerless, afraid, and alone.

But because Uncle Pete showed an interest in me, cared enough to spend time with me and pass on the things his father had taught him (things my pop had never learned), he instilled in me the confidence that I had given away by being unconsciously "obedient" to a code of conduct that had stripped me of my spirit and made me into much less than I was capable of becoming.

It would be years before I would recover most of the spirit that was taken from me.

The next day, while I watched Uncle Pete work on the scooter and handed him tools, he cut out a piece of that beautiful tail section and welded a small pickup bed onto the back of the Cushman. I was now officially in business, since, with the new pickup bed welded in place, I could stack my newspapers and throw them as I cruised down the sidewalks of San Francisco on my early-morning route.

After he was through welding and grinding, he painted the tail section with primer. Later that day, he shot the finish coat, a maroon that matched the original color perfectly.

I had to get the scooter home from Fresno to San Francisco, a trip of about one hundred and eighty miles and, in those days, about three or four hours, depending on how many breaks you took. But that was at a normal speed of sixty miles an hour. The top speed on my new scooter was forty-five miles an hour, give or take.

I was scared. I assured Pop that I could drive it home. Mom was freaked out. I convinced them I could do it. So, at age twelve, with no driver's license but with the basic Doodlebug skills under my belt, I was ready.

We took off from Fresno early on a Wednesday morning and cara-vanned up old Highway 99 with me in the lead, maxed out at forty-five miles an hour, pointed north, hair on fire, leaning into the wind like an old, red Labrador.

Mom and Pop followed close behind in the family boat, a gray 1948 Plymouth four-door sedan. Not once did the California Highway Patrol (seldom seen in those days) give me a nod.

All went well. The day after we arrived home, I set out delivering my early-morning paper route down the sidewalks of the Sunnyside District of San Francisco.

I was instantly one of the top dogs in the neighborhood with that Cushman. I rode the wheels off it for the next three years.

After building my route up by a hundred customers or so because of my new efficiency, it was once again clear that I needed something bigger and faster. The seeds of speed had been planted, and I needed to till the soil.

CHAPTER 3
THE BEATER

I bought my first car at age fifteen, though I should I say I pressured Pop to let me buy it with my saved paper-route money. Pop didn't know it, but it was now payback time for him. When I was younger, he made what he thought was an empty promise: He told me I could have anything I wanted as long as I paid for it. Now that I was able to pay for a car with my paper-route earnings, I was going to hold him to his promise.

Unfortunately, because I absorbed this lesson from Pop, later in life I was unable to accept things such as love, gifts, or offers of help without feeling like I had to pay for them. Feeling like I had to pay my way was a way of devaluing myself; if I wasn't good enough just the way I was, I always felt like I had to do something or be somebody other than who I really was, to make up for who I felt I wasn't. This meant I couldn't just be myself. I found myself often having to fabricate a story to make myself look better in the eyes of others.

This is why I'd say yes when people asked me if I flew in the military. I always hoped they wouldn't pry any further, but if they did ask me, "What did you fly?" then I would either come up with some kind of false proof, or I would admit that, yeah, I flew, but only as an enlisted crewmember.

This car would be my ticket to ride; it would propel me to my first experience of true freedom.

When I found the little, black Ford two-door sedan on Market Street, a couple of doors west on Market from the ever-popular Café Du Nord in San Francisco, I told the car salesman that I wanted the car. I put down five dollars as a deposit. (I remember that guy. He sold used cars during the week and then raced hardtops—stripped-down jalopies—on the weekend at the local Bay Area oval tracks.)

I guess I was so passionate about the little, black two-door that he actually took the deposit. The next day, after Pop got home from work, I dragged him down to the used-car lot.

I had to have this car; she was a 1937 black Ford V8, a V60 sedan. She had an original Ford-factory-installed, sixty horsepower V8 engine. She had definitely been around the block a few times, but she was going to be mine. She was beautiful.

Pop hesitated signing the pink slip until I reminded him of his promise long ago that I could have anything I wanted, as long as I paid for it.

He had no idea of the power of the call for speed that burned in me, the call that led me from learning to ride the Doodlebug and the Cushman to finding a real car.

This was no longer the bush league, the farm club. I was graduating to the big leagues. This was impressive, to me anyway.

Since I was only fifteen years old when I bought the '37 two-door, I wasn't legally able to drive. There were no learner's permits in those days. You were either a licensed driver or you walked, rode your bicycle, or took the Muni (the San Francisco Municipal Railway).

I promised Pop that if he let me buy the car, I would only work on it in front of the house. I had no idea what I was going to do with the car. I had no idea that it would become my hot-rod "boot camp," where I would develop the skills, reflexes, and racing discipline that would help me beat most other cars as I went on to claim my spot in the unofficial early San Francisco Bay Area Hot Rod Hall of Fame.

I needed those wheels to continue the process of establishing myself as somebody. I would indeed work on it, and I would learn about the mechanics of it in preparation for the hot rod that I would later build—the little coupe that would eventually establish itself as one of the fastest hot rods in San Francisco in the mid-fifties.

Many kids my age were infected by the '50s hot-rod scene. *Hot Rod* magazine was new in the stores and newspaper stands, and it affected the thinking of many of my young buddies. But not many of us had the chutzpah, or took the time, or had the foresight—or in my case the all-consuming drive—to put the rest of our lives on hold to build our own car. And not many of us would take the underage leap of faith to drive on the streets of San Francisco without a license.

Street racing in the streets of San Francisco was my first break from the iron fist of my pop. It was during this time that I felt like I had some control over the direction of my life. At least I was doing something on my own terms that I wanted to do. The power I felt behind the wheel of a car, with the strength of an engine under my control, was a precursor of my life to come as an airline pilot, at the controls of a Boeing 707 and later-model aircraft, with the lives of two hundred-plus souls in my hands.

I DIDN'T KNOW IT COULDN'T BE DONE

I parked the '37 two-door in front of our house and did, indeed, work on it. I learned the mechanical ins and outs of the car. I worked until late in the evening on many occasions. Neighbors would have to step over the many droplight extension cords that snaked out of our basement into the innards of the little beast. With all the extension cords entering through the side door of the coupe, it looked like she was on some kind of life support.

But it was time to amend the verbal contract that I had made with Pop to "just work on the car." I violated my part of the contract by chauffeuring my buddies on their early-morning paper routes. Once we were through throwing papers, we included speed runs through the city, fine-tuning our fledgling racing skills in the predawn darkness.

We would adjourn to the Great Highway at San Francisco's Ocean Beach to test the car and ourselves. We'd make multiple high-speed runs back and forth along the fog-shrouded Great Highway, practicing speed shifts, double clutching, and doing four-wheel drifts around corners until the little Ford's Maypop tires would almost peel off the rims. Most of these skills would soon become part of our driving and drag-racing repertoire.

After our speed runs, I'd drop my buddies off and head back home, quietly killing the engine a block away from the empty parking place in front of my house.

I'd coast the car silently up to the front of the house, turn the wheel into the curb until I heard the steering wheel lock click into place, open the door, quietly step into the morning dawn, ease the door closed behind me, tiptoe up the first flight of stairs, and slip silently in through the living room window. Our house was too small for me to have my own room, so the living room was my bedroom.

I would gently slide the window closed behind me, slip into bed, and pretend to be asleep when Pop left for work at six thirty. I lived in fear that he would see the engine heat shimmering up from the little '37's hood on his way to work. If he did, he would quickly realize that I had broken my end of the bargain by driving my car on the street without a license, and this could lead to his taking away the keys to my car. He never did find out. Or at least he never said anything if he did.

FORGOTTEN LESSONS

In the years that followed, I forgot the power of persistence, of following my passion and commitment to something bigger than myself that I had possessed as that budding teenage hot-rodder.

I had unconsciously forged a young brotherhood of my buddies. Our all-consuming passion for cars bonded us. In some way, they were able to vicariously live out their own desires of independence and adventure through me. What I lacked growing up at home, I found by being the centerpiece of my little band of teenage buddies.

This talent, this gift of creating community as a substitute for feeling the loneliness and imposed isolation of being a kid, would be a major theme in my life to come.

A much bigger world would soon loom over me with way too many options for me to deal with. Without mature guidance and wisdom from older men, I would end up dabbling in too many things; diluting my God-given talents of writing, community building, and relation-ships; and fueling my never-ending quest for the next big thing.

I became "educated" as I got older, and forgot to listen to my heart and what it really wanted. I also thought that I should put away the toys of my youth, grow up, and do something "respectable." I bought into the idea that building and racing cars wasn't respectable. Maybe some of that came from my own feelings of inferiority; after all, if I could achieve the kind of notoriety and success that I had as a teenage hot-rodder, it must not be that special of a pursuit, right?

Maybe it had nothing to do with respectability; maybe I was being drawn away from cars and toward aviation by the lingering memory of my first flight in that little J3 Cub.

After high school, at age seventeen, I joined the navy and discovered the elixir of flight. Not only did this look more respectable than hot-rodding, it was also an inevitable step in my progression from hot rods to jets to… But God would come later. I was young and invincible; I didn't need God.

It wouldn't be until many years later, at age forty-one, when my third marriage disintegrated, that I realized the depth of my unconscious behavior that led me to jump into marriages without the slightest clue as to who I was or what I was supposed to bring to my partners.

What really puzzled me was reflecting on the obvious love my parents had for each other and how they managed to remain married to each other for over fifty years, and why I had become such a miserable failure when it came to marriage.

Through this long, painful, but necessary process, I would eventually relearn to listen to my heart.

CHAPTER 4
THE DEUCE COUPE

was hooked on speed. Now I just needed some way to support my habit. At age fifteen, I got a job working as a gas-station attendant after school at the Chevron station on Monterey Boulevard, a few blocks away from my home on Flood Avenue and close to San Francisco City College.

During the year after I bought the '37, which I called the "Beater," and was working on it, I devoured every early-generation *Hot Rod* magazine I could get my hands on. What I discovered was the rising popularity of the 1932 Ford five-window coupe; it was known in hot-rod circles as one of the versions of the iconic Deuce Coupe.

I became friends with a man in my neighborhood who was rebuilding a 1932 Ford roadster in his basement. Bud was older than me, probably in his early thirties at the time. He was a plumber who lived a few blocks away down on Forester Avenue, just a half-block south of Monterey Boulevard. Bud was kind and generous, but he was a rather strange-looking little man. He had a semi-invalid mother who needed a lot of his attention. Her need for attention would be enough that he would never marry.

I used to think, *If only a woman could see into his heart and know what a good man he was, she would realize he would make a good husband.*

He took a liking to me, as I did to him. He took me along when he went looking for parts for his roadster down in "junkyard alley," Evans Street in the Bayview District of San Francisco. I admired his skill at welding and fabricating tools and parts for his car by hand. I had never been taught those skills.

On one of those trips, we stopped by to see George, one of Bud's hot-rod friends. George was rebuilding a beautiful 1932 Ford two-door sedan.

George knew where there was a 1932 Model B five-window Ford coupe with a blown engine. The Model B was the four-cylinder version of the Deuce Coupe. It had an improved version of the engine used in the Model A. But Ford also began producing a very similar car with their new flathead V8 engine. The 1932 V8 car was marketed as the Model 18, though it is now commonly called the Ford V8. Other than the engine, it was virtually indistinguishable from the Model B.

George gave Bud and me some rough directions on where he had seen the broken five-window coupe. It was sitting in the street on the route of the number 10 Municipal Railway bus line that I used to ride to and from St. Paul's, my grammar school in the Mission district. I had ridden that bus every school day from fifth to eighth grade.

Bud and I drove over to see it. As soon as we turned the corner and I saw it parked in front of the owner's house, tires flat, dust and dirt covering it, I fell in love.

When I think back to that day, I realize that seeing that car sitting there was like seeing an apparition of the Virgin Mary. It's inconceivable that it sat there as long as it did, waiting for me to come and own it. It was less than two miles away from my home.

Bud helped me negotiate with the old man who owned it. Seventy-five dollars, once again, and it would be mine.

Bud and I drove back to his house, got a towrope, and pulled the coupe back to my house. Now I had two cars that I would have to convince my pop to let me keep and work on. My passion and vision for what this little Ford could become blocked out any hesitation about where I was going to keep this new addition to my stable.

This car was by no means even as fast in its stock condition as my '37 two-door V8. I had been so brainwashed by the hundreds of *Hot Rod* magazines I had consumed that I knew owning a Deuce Coupe would catapult me into a high status amongst my buddies, and probably more than a few girls, that was totally unattainable with the '37 two-door.

In retrospect, the status I would attain was more in my own mind than in anyone else's.

I had a vision; I saw how, with a little ingenuity, some money, a lot of luck, a few hand tools, and lots of hard work, this would be the car that would make me special for the first time in my life.

The die was cast. When I told Pop I was going to put the Coupe in our basement to tear it down and work on it, he went ballistic.

"God damn it, I told you you could have that other black junker, but this is too much! Where the hell are you going to fit this thing?"

I convinced him there was space for the '32 in the basement if I just removed a section of the wall that separated the space where he parked his car from an adjacent section of the garage. Then I could park it perpendicularly to his car.

"What the hell! You're going to tear out part of the wall?"

"Yeah, Pop, once I get it in there, I won't be taking it out for a long time, so it won't be in the way of you taking your car out in the morning to go to work."

I just kept talking until I wore him down. He agreed to let me put the Deuce Coupe into the basement while the '37 two-door stayed parked curbside.

A TWO-YEAR HIBERNATION

I tore out part of the latticework that separated one section of the basement from the other. I bounced the coupe around and squeezed it into the space I had cleared.

It was tight, but when I needed to work on the '32, I would ask Pop to pull his car out into the street. I would then roll the Coupe out into the space that Pop's car had occupied. That way I had more room to work on my car.

Out came the old Model B four-cylinder engine. Off came the body from the frame rails. I had no idea at the time how, or if, I would finish that project. All I knew was that I had to do it. Little did I know that this car would become one of the fastest hot rods that San Francisco had seen.

The vision of my racing future was fueled by the hundreds of photos and stories I had consumed in those early-era *Hot Rod* magazines. This was finally going to be my chance to be somebody, to have some kind of status that I never had growing up.

TRUE PASSION

If only I had the passion, the drive, and the focus now that I had then. The beauty of being young was, I didn't know that I couldn't do it.

The project was all-consuming. Up until I was old enough to legally drive, I would chase parts for the Deuce Coupe project on my Cushman scooter.

Once I was old enough and I passed my driver's test, the '37 two-door devolved from predawn racer to parts-runner overnight. It became the junkyard shuttle dog between the local yards down at Third Street and Evans Street and Pop's basement.

I didn't know it at the time, and neither did the girls I would soon invite into the inner sanctum of the little, black '37, but the '37 was the forerunner to my little Deuce Coupe—my "rolling fornicatorium"—wherein I would entertain the young ladies who were attracted to the power of a fast car and its driver.

By now, the five-window Deuce lay in a thousand different numbered parts hanging from the basement ceiling and spread systematically through the little space that I had to work in.

I would build the engine using parts mostly acquired from midnight auto suppliers. (Midnight auto suppliers were the nighttime gang of bandit mechanics who roamed the streets looking for autos with the most desirable, and profitable, engine and body parts du jour that the hot-rodders of the day were using. Then they would "chop" the car into parts—engine, transmission, differential, etc.—and sell the pieces to kids like me.)

After I finished scraping, sand blasting, and painting the frame, I reattached the car's body back onto it. There was much more work to do, machining the 1937 Cad LaSalle transmission, so it would mate up with the 1956 Oldsmobile 88 V8 engine and 1940 Ford 4:11 differential. There were countless other tasks that would take the better part of two years and hundreds of dollars to complete.

Once a night's work was done, I would drag the driver's seat up into the Coupe's cab, put a bolt through the seat bracket, secure it to the floorboard, and tighten it. Then I would sit behind the wheel for hours, making engine noises and practicing the speed shifts that would enable me to soon beat most every car I would race in the year to come.

The late nights working at the gas station, the all-consuming work on the '32 in the basement, the missed football practices, and my declining studies were all part of the price I was paying to build and race my dream.

CHAPTER 5

PUTTING THE PEDAL
TO THE METAL

One night, I had an argument with Pop over my breach of his "no grinding, no noise in the basement" after-hours regulation. Something about that confrontation made me realize that the world of difference between the two of us would possibly never be bridged.

Yes, I violated one of Pop's rules that I had agreed to. But it was in the way he seemed to berate me, that he seemed to take his anger out on me, that made me feel I was flawed, not just that I had done something wrong. I felt I was somehow inherently bad, that I didn't matter, that I was insignificant.

This was a continual theme in our relationship; him expressing his frustration through the leaky filter of his anger.

This would be a chasm which neither one of us would be able to cross until many years later. That night, I packed a few things into a duffle bag and called a couple of my buddies to see if they would run away with me. They must have had better home lives than me because they declined.

I threw the bag in the '37 and drove around the city for a few hours, thinking about the life I took for granted that I was running away from. I ended up driving the '37 just three blocks away from my home. I parked up on Ridgewood Avenue, on the hill above Monterey Boulevard, draped myself across the front seat, and tried to sleep. I froze all night.

The next morning, I decided to go back to school in an attempt to coerce some of my buddies to run farther away than three blocks with me. As I drove up in front of school, Pop was waiting there for me. He came running up to my car, jumped on the running board, and pleaded with me to come home. He told me he didn't remember what he had said, but that he was sorry for getting angry with me for my violating one of his noise rules in the basement that night.

I rammed the '37 into first gear, and as I burned rubber away from my high school, I saw Pop lurch back onto the sidewalk after being thrown off the running board.

As I drove down Phelan Avenue and turned west onto Ocean Avenue, I slowed to fifteen miles an hour. I reflected on what I had just done; I felt a deep sadness that I had hurt him—that I couldn't respond to his awkward attempt at an apology.

It would be years later, when I would be able to uncover the love that I did have for him, that I would understand what a good man he was, and how much he meant to so many of the people whose lives he had touched in ways that he was never capable of revealing to me.

I returned home that night. Even though my teenage mind didn't understand what I had done, I knew that rebellious act was a necessary part of my establishing some kind of my own desperate independence from my family.

TEST FLIGHT

It was almost two years to the day from the time that I rolled the Coupe into the basement that I rolled it out. It was not finished by any means, but it was finished enough to slake my thirst for birthing this car onto the Bay Area street-racing scene. I needed to know if this thing would run—really run. I had stripped most of the original wiring out of her. I rewired it to handle the 1956 Oldsmobile electrical system and its components.

Once I got the engine running and did a few shakedown runs through the neighborhood and down Phelan Avenue—my favorite test track in the relatively deserted streets of 1957—I realized the acceleration force of the Oldsmobile engine in this much lighter car caused the big, stock four-barrel carburetor to surge and stumble.

I rejetted and fine-tuned the four-barrel carburetor to stop the fuel surging under acceleration. I continued the shakedown runs the length of Phelan Avenue, the Great Highway at Ocean Beach, Sloat Boulevard, Skyline Boulevard, Brotherhood Way, and the other early-era, impromptu San Francisco drag strips that were so well known to early hot-rodders.

When the kinks were worked out, and the neighbors tired of hearing me incessantly blipping the throttle with the exhaust header pipes uncorked and tuning the engine in the driveway in front of my basement, I was off to the drag strips.

It was more than a car and a race for me; looking back, I realize it was as much about my passion for speed as it was my needing to know if I had enough of the right stuff to be a man.

The fifties car scene just happened to be the launch pad for my vehicle of transformation.

THE YELLOW DRAGON WAGON

I drove my Deuce Coupe to The Little Bonneville drag strip in San Jose for my first officially sanctioned drag race. My buddy, and only pit crewman, Eddie, came with me.

I advanced through the time trials of the A Gas class during the long day of racing, beating everyone I raced.

Late that afternoon, I eased the Coupe up to the starting line, next to the other car that had battled its way to the finals in my class, the Catalina Racing team's big, yellow, blown (supercharged) Chrysler Hemi-powered '48 Ford Business Coupe. I nicknamed it the Yellow Dragon Wagon.

The two cars were total contrasts in style, preparation, and financing. My little five-window's fuselage was painted a deep Baltic blue, but its fenders were still a dull, flat-black primer.

My racing budget was minimal at best. It was financed by the savings from my former paper route and my after-school and weekend work at the gas station.

I decided to forgo the finish coat of paint and dedicate what little money and time I had left to putting the long project to the race test.

Time was running short, since I was coming up on high school graduation, and the navy had plans for the next two years of my life. I had
joined the navy reserves early in my junior year of high school, so I
already knew I'd serve two years active duty upon graduating.

I was afraid that I wouldn't be able to put the '32 on the street in
time before I had to report for active duty. I needed to prove that the
two years I had put into building her would finally pay off. I needed to
justify the sacrifices I had made during that time. I needed to know the
blind faith I had in building my car was going to amount to something.

I blipped the throttle a few times. I loved the sound of the now-
uncorked header pipes emitting noise that the laws of the street
prevented.

The big hulk of the yellow '48 idling next to me was the epitome of
the word *polish*. The racing team had pushed it to the line with a matching yellow pickup truck. Inside, the driver wore a matching yellow
helmet and coveralls.

As the driver let out the clutch to start the big Hemi en route to the
starting line, the '48 belched flames out of the brightly chromed Laker
pipes running aft and exiting just forward of the fat racing slicks on the
rear tires.

The ground shook when the engine lit off. The driver blipped the
throttle a few times to bring the heart of the beast to life.

My pitman, Eddie, was a longtime neighborhood pal. He would go
on to build one of the notable neighborhood rods—a '40 Ford Business
Coupe with one of the earliest Chevy 283-cubic inch V8 transplants
that would later become commonplace on the streets of San Francisco.

I sat there in my car, engine idling, headers uncorked. I could feel
every pulsation of that big, rocket-powered Super 88 V8 Oldsmobile
engine. Man, I knew every valve, every lifter, every connecting rod that
was rotating or moving in that engine block.

I had worked on, polished, and breathed life into every part that was
now idling smoothly two feet in front of me.

Eddie ran frantically from one side of the Coupe to the other as he
wiped a carbon tetrachloride-soaked rag around the rear, gum-rubber
Bruce's racing slicks. This would soften the gummy tread for maximum
traction.

Besides, less wheel spin meant a few more speed runs before I had to make a trip across the bay to Hayward to pop for new racing slicks.

REFLEX ACTION

As word spread over the two years that I had been working on the '32 that something hot was brewing in the basement over at 521 Flood Avenue, I accumulated a bunch of gearhead buddies.

Along with my buddies, Dave Bostrom, Jim Humphries, and Bob McAfee (Stubbie), I spent countless hours in Humph's basement, sitting in front of the wooden box that contained the red, yellow, and green lights, one of the first "Christmas-tree" lighting systems known to drag racing. The box was jury-rigged to act as a "reflex trainer" for our motley racing crew. (We called ourselves the Botta, Bostrom, Stubbie, and Humph Racing Team.)

One kid would punch a button that would start the contraption counting down, with the red light changing to yellow and then to green, while the other one would hit the starter's watch, measuring the time it took for the third kid, seated in a beat-up old La-Z-Boy with a spring or two popping through the mottled, dark brown vinyl, to lift his right foot from the brake pedal and stomp on the throttle. It wasn't scientific, but it did improve our reaction times.

This was all carefully designed to fine-tune the hardwiring between the designated kid's adolescent, reptilian brain and his quivering right foot.

For the first time in my life, I had a shot at taking control of something that made sense to me, something that had the unmistakable smell of my own kind of greasy manhood smeared all over it.

A RACE FOR THE FUTURE

I glanced to my right again, and in my peripheral vision, I saw the Dragon. The body of the Dragon was rocking back and forth in tune with a full race camshaft, whose valve timing superimposed on a graph would make the Dow Jones Industrial Average look like code blue on a cardio machine.

The flagman looked over at me and tipped the green starting flag in my direction. I took his acknowledgment to heart, as if he were encouraging me to win this race for every other kid who wanted to be his own man.

I nodded to the flagman and eased my black-and-white tennie off the brake pedal and down onto the five-window Coupe's original, little, spoon-shaped chrome throttle pedal. I glanced up at the tachometer, mounted, like a gun sight, high and in the center of the little Coupe's dashboard.

Once the revs were dialed in at twenty-five hundred, I hesitated for just a split second; I needed to synch up every fiber in my body to the sound and the feel of the big Olds engine, vibrating now at launch speed. Only then did I shift my gaze to the starter's right arm, while my ass now vibrated in synch with the 324-cubic inch power plant in front of me.

My laser-like gaze penetrated his arm, searching for the slightest twitch that would trigger the synapses in my brain to launch my two-year project down the quarter mile of asphalt in front of me.

Every fiber in my body was ready, poised to slam 155 pounds of teenage, hot-rod passion down onto that shiny little spoon until it came out the radiator, if need be.

This was the first test, for both the '32 and me. This was the first day her slicks had touched an official drag strip. I had tested her thoroughly during my various unofficial street races. Even though this was our first official race, I was ready. I didn't know it at the time, but I was launching my dream of flight into tomorrow, off of that 1,320-foot strip stretched out in front of me.

This was the time when I would make my mark as a kid to be reckoned with, as someone who mattered. Over the last two years, I had been building my significance as I built my car. I needed to go out in a blaze of glory before Uncle Sam nabbed me for my two years of mandatory naval service.

My plan was paying off, belying the fact that I had pretty much built the Deuce Coupe—with the blueprinted 324-cubic inch, 240 horsepower, 350 ft-lbs of torque, '56 Olds engine, '37 Cadillac/LaSalle transmission and stock, and '40 Ford 4:11 differential—with a tool kit that was definitely south of sophisticated, to put it mildly.

LAUNCH TIME

The flagman slowly pointed to my Coupe and then to the dragon. In that split second, as I waited for the slightest twitch of the flagman's arm, I thought of the long hours sitting in front of that wooden reflex box, and everything that I had done in prepping the Coupe for this moment blurred.

In one fluid motion, I dumped the clutch and drove the shiny spoon into a permanent indentation on the Coupe's floor mat. As I expected, based on the impromptu street races leading up to this moment, my Deuce Coupe got the hole-shot (jump) on the big, yellow sled.

The revs leaped from twenty-five hundred to five thousand in a nanosecond, accompanied by shrill screams from the soft gum rubber of the 800- by 17-inch slicks. They were doing their damndest to excavate the asphalt from the starting line.

The screams from the spinning slicks melded into the roar emitting from the Coupe's uncorked header plugs, producing a delicious cacophony that can only be fully appreciated by those who have attended this kind of symphony before.

For an instant, the conflict between what was right and what I had to do to put my car on the track and my life in some kind of order flashed through my mind. The karmic payback had long ago been established through my dealings with the devil at midnight auto supply.

I had two hundred feet on the Dragon by the time I passed the first eighth of a mile. Then I looked in the rearview mirror.

With what would become a familiar, sickening recognition in my ongoing duel with the Hemi-powered Dragon at future races, I saw the smooth, yellow molded nose of the Dragon just beginning to emerge from the shroud of acrid, blue smoke that had enveloped the car, as it began to outrace its self-generated mushroom cloud of burning rubber.

The yellow '48 was gobbling up big chunks of race track in its attempt to catch me by the time we would roar through the time traps, which were now less than an eighth of a mile ahead.

My lead was being reeled in faster than Julia Child's would be in a tug-of-war with Hulk Hogan.

I glanced at the tach as the needle nailed five grand. In one hair-splitting, coordinated move, I stomped hard on the clutch pedal and slammed the long shift lever that snaked up out of the Cad/LaSalle's box down, mercilessly, into its third and final gear.

I heard the sound of a slider shaft being slammed around violently deep inside the bulletproof gearbox. The little Coupe lurched hard from left to right with the sudden shift in the engine's thrust vector.

The noise of that gear slamming around in the box triggered my fear that the motor mounts holding the big Olds in place would be ripped away from the spindly little Coupe's frame due to the massive torque being generated.

If that happened, the engine would corkscrew its way out of the frame and onto the drag strip, pulling the Coupe along behind it, spiraling, like the remains of a potato hanging from a peeler.

I flashed back to Gus's radiator shop in Daly City where I'd had the motor mounts, necessary to bolt the humongous Olds engine into the tiny Coupe's frame, welded in place. Man, I cursed the fact that I ran short of the needed cash from my gas-station job to properly gusset the Coupe's frame to handle the torque of the big Olds mill.

THE LAST WIN

The finish line was coming up fast. I prayed to the god of Speed, the only one that I knew at the time, "Please, God, let me win this one! If you do, I'll do anything, anything that you want!"

I crossed the line a split second ahead of the yellow tub. My elapsed time was milliseconds quicker than the Dragon's, but the difference in our top speeds was a massive twenty miles per hour in the Dragon's favor.

Just as I crossed the line, the big '48 blew by on my right. As if to punctuate the message that it was time for me to upgrade my car or look for another line of work, the weight and speed differential between the two cars crossing the line at almost the same moment created a vortex that pulled violently on the little Coupe and almost sucked it into the monster's wake.

I cranked the steering wheel hard to the left to keep the Coupe from being sucked into the '48's draft.

We won. But it was too close for comfort. As soon as I clocked through the speed traps, I felt a wave of empathy for my little Coupe's engine. I punched the clutch in and coasted the rest of the way down the strip to the turnoff lane leading back to the pits.

Eddie came running up and jumped on the running board to congratulate me. I was quiet for a moment. Then I said, "I don't know Eddie, whaddya think? Where'm I gonna get the money ta stay ahead of these guys? I'm puckerin' every time I look in the mirror and see that tub closin' on me."

"Ah, Bert, no sweat. You can work more hours at the station and, besides, there's a lot of cubes left inside the Olds. You can bore it out, get a stroker kit and..."

"Hey, man, I can't do it. You know we're about to graduate, and then the navy wants my ass for a few years. C'mon, get in; we'll go talk about it in the pits."

Eddie said, "Did you see the look on those guys' faces, man? They couldn't believe it. You beat their asses! That's so far out, man. They trailer the car down here, have all those guys with the fancy, monogrammed uniforms in the pits, checkin' the engine, changin' this and that. We drive the Coupe here, uncork the headers, mess with the four-barrel a little bit, and go out and kick ass on the... the... Racing Team, man!"

What made this first test against the Yellow Dragon's racing team so important, with my newly built Coupe right out of the box, was that I won against a deck that seemed to be stacked against me.

If I had stopped to think about what I had to do to beat this car and its racing team, I never would have begun the project. I didn't know it could be done, but I did it anyway.

For the few months remaining before I had to report for active duty,

I raced the '32 at other drag strips around the Bay Area. I continued to improve the little Coupe's elapsed times in the quarter-mile races from the low fourteen seconds into the high thirteens. But it wasn't the same.

I was out of money, and my winning days were numbered because of the navy nipping at my heels. Both Eddie and I knew the end was near, but neither one of us wanted to talk about it.

And though it was the end of an era, my need for speed was only just beginning to rear its head; it would soon take a different form.

CHAPTER 6

THE ELIXIR OF FLIGHT

During my junior and senior years in high school, when I was building the little Deuce Coupe, I was also playing navy reservist by attending "drill nights" at Treasure Island Naval Station, in the middle of San Francisco Bay. Treasure Island is a manmade island halfway between San Francisco and Oakland. It was built in 1936 and '37 for the Golden Gate International Exposition. It also anchors one of the mid spans of the San Francisco/Oakland Bay Bridge. Subsequent to the fair's closing, Treasure Island was commissioned a naval base.

I made a deal with Uncle Sam that, upon graduation from high school, I'd put in two years of active duty and then finish up my military obligation with another three years of reserve duty upon return to civilian life.

During my basic training at the U.S. Naval Training Station in San Diego, California, I'd spot the little green stripes on the other enlisted men's uniforms that designated the naval aviation division of the enlisted corps.

Something about airplanes and flying flashed through my mind the moment I saw those green stripes.

I figured being around airplanes would be better and more exciting than consistently losing my lunch aboard some tin can in the middle of the Atlantic Ocean. (*Tin can* is navy lingo for the ship known as a destroyer.) So I requested aviation training and got it. In July 1957, less than a month after graduating from high school and putting the Coupe in mothballs, I was sent to Norman, Oklahoma.

In Norman, I got a crash course in basic aviation terminology, air-craft handling, physics, trigonometry, and a bunch of other stuff that I had to study like crazy to absorb. We even got to stand behind an early-generation jet aircraft (I think it was an F-86) as it ran its engine up to about 80 percent thrust to see what effect it would have on us if we absentmindedly walked behind one of these beasts on the flight line or carrier deck.

I was also initiated into southern heat, humidity, and huge flying cockroaches, which I had never experienced before.

Once I got to Norman, I found out that I had the necessary quali-fying GCT (General Classification Test) scores to apply for NavCad (Navy Cadet) pilot training. But as an insecure teenager and airman apprentice, I didn't have a very good opinion of myself, so I declined the opportunity to apply.

Meanwhile, some of my enlisted buddies, who also qualified for NavCad training, accepted the challenge to be tested. They went to Pensacola, Florida, took the NavCad tests, passed them, and received a pilot class soon after.

To add insult to injury, some months later, these same guys came through Barin Field, Alabama, one of the outlying World War II air-bases that made up the navy's Pensacola Training Command, where I was stationed as an apprentice electronics technician. They were instrument and navigation pilot trainees.

They wasted no time in rubbing it in, in a good-natured way, that I was some kind of idiot for not having taken the NavCad test.

I joked back with them, but they had no idea how painful it was for me to see them climb into their flight suits and go out for a hop in their T-28 trainers.

Deep down inside the insecure teenager, there was a sleeping giant, and with each missed opportunity, something inside me was awaken-ing. But still, because of that missed opportunity to be initiated into what at the time appeared to be my only version of "the right stuff," I would carry that pain of not feeling like a "real pilot" for much of my early airline flying career.

At Barin, I was assigned to the radio shop, where I apprenticed as an electronics technician, working on radio gear in the basic training aircraft, such as the T-28, the SNJ, and the SNB that the Navy used at that time to train fledgling aviators.

It was there at Barin that the budding young naval aviators were being taught instrument flying, navigation, and carquals (aircraft carrier qualification).

It was also there that I began to form my hero worship for naval aviators and their flying machines. I don't know whether it was because I felt like I could never do what they were doing, or because I felt such a reverence for what they had to go through to get their wings. Regardless, that hero worship would stay with me for the rest of my aviation career and beyond.

I felt a deep need to learn from, and be mentored by, these men, some of whom were only a few years older than me.

When I allowed myself to go there in my mind, I wondered what it would be like to be one of those supermen.

That vision was so far from what I had known growing up under my father's rule that I couldn't even imagine it.

MENTOR IN A POOPY SUIT

During my time as an impressionable teenage airman apprentice, I began to watch other men. I observed them because I thought if I could figure out how they did things, then I could emulate them.

I especially watched the officers. I wanted to be one because they looked like they were in control of their lives. They were intelligent, were respected, and seemed to be more generally informed than the enlisted men were. I didn't think I was smart enough to be one, though.

There was one officer who stood out above the rest. If he hadn't come into my life at that time, I would have had to invent him. He embodied everything I thought I wanted to be, and in the end, I lost him before I truly even got to know him.

The officer was a young LTJG (lieutenant, junior grade) named McGill. If you were picking a candidate for a *Top Gun* role depicting a typical naval aviator, McGill would be your man. He stood about five-foot-ten, weighed about 160 pounds, and had oceanic blue eyes and light, sandy brown hair.

Something about his face, in total contrast to that of the sternness of my pop's face and mine, made him one of the most pleasant, approachable men I would ever meet.

He was a couple of years older than me, and he was a NavCad graduate. Prior to pilot training, he had attended Princeton, but had left after two years. McGill busted any image I might've had about aloof Ivy League school kids.

McGill used to tell the enlisted men that he liked "hitting the beach" (going on liberty) with us better than with the officers because he had more fun. I suspect he said that to make us feel better about ourselves. That's the kind of guy he was.

I started working alongside McGill after I got orders to leave Barin Field in 1958 for VS39 (antisubmarine squadron 39) in Quonset Point, Rhode Island. VS39 was readying their pilots and aircraft to deploy aboard the USS *Randolph*, a CVS-class aircraft carrier (Invincible class, ASW Antisubmarine warfare carrier) from its home base in Norfolk, Virginia.

After arriving at Quonset, I spent a few months finding my niche in the squadron and preparing for my first deployment to the North Atlantic.

When VS39 deployed to the *Randolph*, it was to qualify our pilots for carrier landings (carquals) in the North Atlantic. We flew the S2-F Tracker, affectionately known as "Stuuf," a Grumman-built, propeller-driven antisubmarine aircraft with relatively sophisticated onboard electronic submarine detection and tracking gear.

Our squadron was the first propeller-driven aircraft that the *Randolph*'s ship's company had seen, since the carrier had just been converted from an attack (CVA) carrier with jet aircraft to an antisub (CVS) carrier with ASW (antisubmarine warfare) prop planes.

No one knows for sure what happened, but it's presumed that some crewmember spilled a five-gallon bucket of aircraft engine oil on the deck the night before the early-morning launch. Either no one saw it, or they neglected to clean it up.

Once the launch got underway in the black, North Atlantic predawn, the "shooter," or the officer in charge of launching aircraft, waved his red battery-powered wands at McGill's aircraft as a signal to taxi forward to take his position on the starboard catapult.

I was standing off to one side of McGill's aircraft as I saw the dark silhouette of McGill's right hand reach up to the overhead throttle quadrant in the Stuuf's cockpit.

He rocked the throttle levers on the two big R2800 radial engines carefully back and forth as he inched them forward just enough to move his aircraft into position onto the catapult.

The noise from the two big radials was lost in the hurricane of wind and a thousand other sounds that engulf the flight deck of an aircraft carrier during flight operations.

As McGill turned his aircraft to line up with the catapult, his Stuuf's prop wash, in combination with the carrier completing its turn into the wind, forced me into a thirty-degree lean against an instant gale force.

The sharp red flames emanating from the Stuuf's exhaust stacks a mere ten feet away from where I stood licked at me like the devil's tongue. Besides the exhaust glow, the pencil-like red wands of the "shooter" were all that was visible in the silky, black predawn.

McGill taxied his Stuuf over the oil slick, and as the deck pitched left, his aircraft began a sickening, synchronistic, slow-motion skid toward the port side of the flight deck.

I stood there, frozen in anguished disbelief, as an impotent cry of "Mac!" was ripped from my lips and lost to the chaos of what was unfolding.

Mac's Stuuf, with him and a full crew—copilot and two enlisted electronic countermeasures experts, crammed into their seats amidst thousands of pounds of electronic gear—cartwheeled lazily over the left side of the carrier's flight deck.

She took thirty feet of catwalk (the walkway surrounding most of the ship, immediately below the flight deck) with her, landing topside down.

As she hit the water, she looked like an inverted sperm whale, flipped on its back, with her still-extended landing gear pointed awkwardly skyward. Her white belly, barely visible in the inky blackness, shone phosphorescent as she began to slip beneath the waves tugging at her fuselage.

The frantic spinning of her propellers seemed to act in her fatal favor as she churned her way through the water's surface, seeking a frothy grave in the frigid, angry waters of the North Atlantic.

We lost all four men. The last time I saw what was left of McGill was about six hours later as the "angel," the recovery helicopter, deposited some of the four crewmembers' recovered gear down onto the flight deck.

I looked down at the gear and saw McGill's "poopy suit," the rubber exposure suit that the navy required all crewmembers operating flights over cold water to wear, flapping in the wind blowing across the carrier deck.

It was ripped to shreds. McGill's name was written in large black letters on one of the larger pieces of the suit.

In some strange, immeasurable way, LTJG McGill helped initiate the healing process of my teenage future-aviator's soul. He also fanned the small flame of possibility that I might someday be worthy enough to fly airplanes.

McGill left an indelible impression on me of what real manhood and leadership was about: being vulnerable, fun-loving, open, and strong, and yet, being respectful of and honoring younger men. He modeled the man I wanted to be in his love for life, his passion for flight. I've never forgotten him.

Maybe that's why I still harbor a special place in my heart for naval aviators to this day.

CHAPTER 7
THE NAIL IN THE COFFIN

Shortly after McGill's death, I took a thirty-day leave and went home to San Francisco. I didn't know it at the time, but I would be attending the funeral of my Deuce Coupe once I got there.

When I got to my parents' house, I immediately went down to the basement and gently pulled the faded old green bedsheet off of the little five-window Deuce Coupe. The sheet glided easily over the twenty coats of shiny Baltic blue lacquer paint covering the tall, straight cab of the Coupe.

As the sheet slid to the floor, I turned slowly around in a full circle. I stared at the rough-cut, fuzzy redwood lath and plastered walls of Pop's basement as if I might extract some answers for my life lying hidden in the catacombs that had spawned my escape vehicle a few short years before.

I reeled with the changes in my life that had wrenched me from the simple world of hot rods, street racing, and chicks in the short span of a year. I was contemplating my future as an adult in a world that didn't have time or space anymore for a kid and his five-window Deuce Coupe.

I ran my hand over the big, white-sidewall street tire on the left rear wheel. Then I reached in through the rumble seat and attached the battery cables that were hanging loose in the trunk. I walked around to the driver's side door, opened it, and slowly slid onto the original light brown fuzz-upholstered seat.

I reached up and put my left hand on the original spindly little '32 Ford steering wheel, and with my right hand, I hit the starter button, implanted neatly below the original oval-shaped, burnished-aluminum dashboard.

The 240 horsepower, blueprinted Olds engine, that for the last year had lain dormant under the split-sided hood of the Deuce Coupe, roared to life on the first crank.

My eyes darted immediately to the oil pressure gauge, as the clean, honey-colored engine oil rose quickly to sixty PSI.

"God damn it, shut that thing off," Pop's voice bellowed down through the sheet-metal heating pipe from his throne, the couch in the living room. I flipped off the ignition switch. The oil pressure gauge dropped back to zero as fast as it had risen.

"Son of a bitch," I cursed the old man for many things, but this time for my not being allowed to nurture my long-neglected relationship with my little blue soul mate.

POP'S HOUSE

My pop was a tough old Italian: strict, unforgiving, emotionally unavailable, and always hidden behind his cigar, newspaper, and TV after work. I finally figured out after many years that he was afraid of failing if he explored his artistic talents. But his need for security overrode his desire to express his talent, so he swallowed it, only to have it expressed in a lifetime of frustration and regret.

The little boy inside of him was very scared. In addition to whatever other emotional baggage I picked up along the way, I inherited his fear, his restlessness, and his general disdain for himself in not having accomplished what he could have.

To this day, I struggle with what I know I'm good at but hesitate to fully engage in.

Pop wanted nothing other than to be left alone to smoke a few cigars, to watch a little TV after a hard day's work as a chef at one of the leading Italian restaurants in San Francisco, and for the basement to be finally clean of my hot-rod stuff: fenders, spare engine parts, an extra differential assembly—all the usual mechanical detritus that occupies a young gearhead's basement.

A clean basement would be only a figment of the old man's imagination for many years, since the vision I had when I was in high school and building my Deuce Coupe was "Build it, and I will be good enough."

I felt alone after the loss of McGill. I was often afraid, feeling that no one could understand me or give me direction. I would often think of how McGill would have done something, how he would have handled a situation. I often saw his face, smiling, relaxed, as I struggled through challenges in which I was feeling indecisive, or lacking enough knowledge to move forward.

I absentmindedly gave the little hand crank that opened the windshield a couple of turns, closed my eyes, took a deep breath. A tear dripped from the corner of my right eye; I let it fall onto my pants. I looked at it for a long time as it grew into a dark spot on my light-colored khakis. Before I had gone into the navy and had my heart stretched by my loss of McGill, I would have quickly wiped it away.

I slid slowly out of the Coupe, walked over to the wall behind the car, and pulled the phone off the hook; I dialed Eddie's number. When he answered, I cleared my throat and said, "Hey, man, I'm home. Let's go racin'!"

ONE LAST RACE

I made the call to Eddie on a Thursday afternoon, the day I had arrived home from the East Coast. The following morning, I was down in the basement, checking the air in the tires, dropping the Coupe off the jack stands, and changing her oil. I even put a fresh coat of unneeded wax over the shiny blue paint.

That afternoon, Eddie and I called some girls that we thought might still be available. After exhausting both of our address books with nothing panning out, I went back home and showered. Then I drove around the corner and picked Eddie up, and we drove the '32 over to Mel's Drive-in on Van Ness Avenue in San Francisco for a couple of burgers. After we finished eating, we hung out there, waiting to see if anybody we knew came through the drive-in.

About eight o'clock that evening, we pulled out of Mel's and headed down the peninsula. As we cruised down Highway 101, we had a great time talking about the good ol' days of a year long gone.

"Ya know, Ed, it doesn't seem like a year since I've been gone, and yet it feels like a long time. Know what I mean?"

"I hear ya, man! It hasn't been the same without you around here. A lot of the guys are putting the new Chevy 283s in their cars, and everybody's goin' pretty fast. I mean, I ain't sayin' that you wouldn't be able to still beat 'em or nothin', but things have changed, man."

"Yeah, we'll see."

I felt good having the Coupe out of mothballs and driving her again. I pulled off to the side of 101, near the Brisbane exit, and traded seats with Eddie.

"You got it, man. Kibby's." (Kibby's was a drive-in restaurant on El Camino Real in San Mateo where the wannabe hot-rodders from northern and central California hung out.)

Somehow, I knew our time together in the little Deuce Coupe was short. I wanted to share her with my buddy in the hopes that she'd have the same lasting impact on him that she'd had on me.

THE NEON MECCA

We figured that the action on Friday night was still at Kibby's. After trading seats and heading south a few miles, Eddie pulled off 101 at the Third Avenue, San Mateo exit. We headed southwest down Third to El Camino. We hung a left on El Camino and headed south.

A few miles down El Camino, on the south side of the road, glowed Kibby's, a rotating beacon for hot-rodders that shone brightly in the hearts of all those NorCal teenage street racers and wannabes, itching to develop their own versions of the hot-rodders' right stuff.

This was the street racers' neon Mecca. If you made the pilgrimage from Fresno, Stockton, Tracy, Turlock, the City, or Redding; raced; and conquered here, you were assured of a place in the unofficial NorCal Hall of Drag Racing Fame.

Eddie slowed the Coupe to a crawl to avoid scraping her two-inch dropped axle on the driveway as we pulled into Kibby's. All heads turned in recognition of the little blue coupe with the dropped front axle and the big, rear white-walled Goodyears. The kids in their cars, who were still around from the last year, squinted to see who was behind the wheel. Seeing Eddie threw them for a loop. For a moment, they thought I had sold the car.

We cruised slowly around the circular parking lot, checking out who was there and what some of the new rods were sporting. We talked to some of the guys we recognized from a year ago. Eddie said, to no one in particular, "Man, these guys look the same as they did a year ago. And they're talkin' about the same old shit they were then."

Eddie's statement somehow reassured me that I had done the right thing by giving two years of my life to the navy.

Then we saw it, parked at the 180-degree point of the drive-in's circle, with the food tray neatly propped up on the driver's side door—a shiny, new black '57 Corvette convertible with gray trim lining both door recesses. It also had something else: the little, telltale Duntov emblem mounted low on the convertible's fiberglass front fender. If you weren't looking for the emblem, you'd surely miss it. And if you didn't know what it meant, then you didn't understand that this was the latest, fastest version of Chevrolet's Corvette model.

We idled by the 'Vette to check it out. With a nod of his head, the 'Vette driver showed us that he knew who we were. We both knew he was the one we were looking for, even though we had never seen him before.

Some of the guys we saw that night were still coming up from the central valley to be part of the NorCal action at Kibby's. Once most of the guys performed the necessary prerace social rituals and the chicks determined the pecking order of who would ride with whom, they'd adjourn to the unofficial, and highly illegal, street drag-race track up at Cañada Road in Redwood City, to test their equipment against some of NorCal's best. The Friday night ritual was that all the hot-dog racers and wannabes stopped by the drive-in to check out the competition before heading up to Cañada around midnight. Most of the kids drove their cars up there from Kibby's.

A few of the more serious racers trailered their cars up there for a night of unsanctioned drag racing in order to work the bugs out of their machinery in preparation for the weekend's official drags at the many strips that dotted the Bay Area: Little Bonneville at San Jose, Fremont, Hayward, Champion Speedway in Brisbane, and Half Moon Bay, to name a few.

During my time in the navy, I had read all the latest car magazines touting the forthcoming superiority of the new Duntov camshaft-powered, 283-cubic inch Chevy V8. Eddie and I were scanning the crowd for one of the new Chevys that might be sporting the big new V8 with the Duntov camshaft.

The engine specs for the new Chevy engine were daunting: The 1956 Corvette received a 210-horsepower, 265-cubic inch V8; a 225-horsepower, dual four-barrel 265-cubic inch engine; or a special 265-cubic inch engine sporting the infamous "Duntov Cam" resulting in 240 horsepower. The 1957 Corvette received the 283-cubic inch V8 and fuel injection. This marked the first year that fuel injection was available on a Corvette. The idea of fuel injection was Zora Duntov's, and he was responsible for encouraging Chevrolet management to undertake this costly joint venture with Rochester Products. However, the system was ultimately designed and built by John Dolza, another engineer. The 283-cubic inch engine, combined with fuel injection, now had an output of 283 horsepower. The Corvette won the honors of being the first production-based passenger vehicle in the world to sport one horsepower per cubic inch. (Wikipedia)

The new Corvette would probably be driven by one of the local rich boys, whose pop would have bought him some new wheels so he could boast about being the fastest kid on the peninsula—for a month or so, anyway.

We had been regulars at Kibby's up to the time I left for the navy a year before. The Deuce Coupe had won most of her midnight races up at Cañada, so her reputation had preceded her.

The 'Vette driver was seeking the fleeting adulation that adorns the one with the fastest car on the peninsula. It would be the first notch on his racing belt, and possibly the sole reward for being the son of wealthy parents.

This would be his one moment, too—the time when he excelled at something that he did more or less on his own.

While it was impossible for the 'Vette driver to fully appreciate being anointed in the same racing oil that Eddie and I had been, this would also be a rite of passage, of sorts, into manhood for him.

MANDATORY EARLY RETIREMENT

We circled the drive-in lot a couple more times until the kid and his buddy in the 'Vette couldn't stand it any longer. They gulped down their shakes, unscrewed the food tray from the driver's side door, and pitched the tray onto the asphalt parking lot. Before the tray hit the ground, he lit off the 'Vette's engine, and it roared to life.

It was a beautiful machine, and the best that 1957 Hillsborough dollars could buy. As soon as the 'Vette followed us out of the lot and we heard the lope of that fuel-injected Duntov V8, I knew that my racing life would never be quite the same again.

We turned right out of the drive-in lot onto El Camino. The 'Vette was right behind us, a few car lengths back. As soon as Eddie unwound the steering wheel and headed south, the caravan behind the 'Vette swelled to fifteen or twenty of every kind of street and custom rod that epitomized the NorCal hot-rod scene at that magical time. The racing alarm went off in the soul, and the balls, of every kid assembled there.

Whoever won this race tonight would unwittingly provide the rest of these kids with a vicarious personal victory, a collective immersion in the waters of manhood that had been reduced to a trickle for most of them in a society that was bereft of anything remotely resembling a rite of passage.

I looked over my shoulder as Eddie continued to cruise slowly down El Camino. The drive-in lot was now empty, except for the litter of hundreds of bits of french fries and pieces of burger lying wildly askew after being pitched from the dumped food trays they had sat on less than a minute before. God bless the drive-in waitresses, who would clean up after us in service to a higher purpose that night.

FOR WANT OF AN AFTERBURNER

The procession motored slowly down El Camino, stopping reverently at each traffic light along the way. In contrast to the slow speed of the group, the tension to get on it was palpable.

The Friday-night, NorCal hot-rod extravaganza had grown to approximately forty cars. At each stop sign, the kids would chatter to each other out their car windows, choosing sides and convincing each other who would win and why.

Eddie and I were quiet; normally, I would be hunched over the wheel, reviewing the mental tricks that I had learned from the many hours at the wheel of the wooden-box reflex trainer in Humph's basement.

Strategy was important. It might serve our mission better to suggest a "rolling go" on the way up to Cañada road, meaning the two cars that were to race would roll along at about five or ten miles an hour, and upon a hand signal from one of the kids hanging out the window of one of the cars, the race would start.

Or should we start from a dead stop on the stretch of Cañada Road that had been dedicated that night as a drag strip? (This strategy benefited our coupe, since the higher power-to-weight ratio of our car bettered our cause, giving us faster acceleration and a better "hole shot" than the lesser-displacement, lower-torque 'Vette.)

The dead-stop start would gain us immediate distance on our competition, giving me one last time to seek favor from the drag-racing gods.

Eddie pulled up along the right side of the 'Vette; he shouted out the window, "Dead stop go up at Cañada!" The guys in the 'Vette nodded back, conceding the toss to us. This was good. They either must have known this would be our last effort to try to maintain our racing superiority, or they were confident that the big-bucks Duntov 'Vette would be fast enough to drive what would be the final nail into the Deuce Coupe's racing coffin.

TECHNOLOGY OVER GUTS

When the procession arrived at Cañada Road, the faithful knew what to do; they rolled their cars into position along the right hand side of the road. Once they were in place, and at some mystical, predetermined time, like a thousand birds flying in formation know how to turn simultaneously, the headlights came on, lighting the long, straight road ahead. (We borrowed this move from *Rebel Without a Cause*, which had come out a couple of years earlier.)

As Eddie pulled the Coupe up to the unofficial starting line in the middle of the road, I quickly switched seats with him. We looped the big, olive-drab, army-surplus aircraft seat belts and shoulder straps over our heads and buckled in.

Then I eased the Cad LaSalle gearbox into first gear and inched my way up alongside the 'Vette on the imaginary starting line, just like in the movie. It was only the two of us in the middle of the road; the 'Vette in the oncoming lane and us in the right lane. The headlights from the cars lining the road highlighted almost the full stretch out ahead of the Coupe. One of the kids, who had run about two-thirds of the way down the road, marked off what he thought was a quarter mile.

Two of the other kids had driven their cars to the far end of the road and placed wooden barriers that they had borrowed from a construction site in order to prevent any through traffic from penetrating our racetrack.

Another one of the kids stepped out between the Coupe and the Duntov 'Vette. He had a white handkerchief in his hand. But there would be no truce tonight.

He must have watched a lot of drag races because he was good. He pointed to us and then to the 'Vette. I felt the heat from Eddie's body, twenty-four inches to my right. I looked over to check on Eddie's beefy shoulder harness and gave it a protective tug.

A wave of gratitude swept over me for Eddie's loyal friendship; I felt my eyes tear up. The 'Vette driver's buddy was alongside him also, albeit in more plush surroundings.

But their bond couldn't have been as strong as ours in the blue Coupe, having been cemented over the many hours of wrenching and racing together. All the money on the peninsula couldn't buy that kind of friendship.

As the flag kid raised the white handkerchief high in the cool night air, I watched for all the familiar signals, just like I had done so many times before. Simultaneously, with the starter kid's hand twitching, I slipped my foot off the partially engaged clutch and pinned the little chrome spoon to the floor in one violent, practiced move.

I had the 'Vette out of the chute, although I could feel the difference between the big street tires that the Coupe was wearing tonight and the Bruce slicks that she ran at the drag strip.

"Shit, Eddie, we're layin' down way too much rubber!" I screamed at my copilot. To the untrained observer, the Coupe appeared to leap off the line as usual, but to me there was a sluggishness to her as I backed off the throttle just a tad to let the street tires catch some traction off the line.

I got enough bite, though, to have the 'Vette by four car lengths as the Coupe passed the midpoint of the high beams lighting the track.

"We got 'em, Bert, we got 'em!!" Eddie screamed, while looking straight ahead down the dark tunnel that loomed beyond the faithfuls' headlights.

The big mill seemed to sense my desperation. She dug into those cubic inches for max output like I'd never felt before, even as she approached code blue on the tach. I grabbed the snake's neck and slammed it hard, down into third gear, spot-on the five grand disintegration line.

I had to know. I looked up into the little, square rearview mirror hanging from above the coupe's straight windshield. The 'Vette was closing fast on the left. We were just about out of track lighting, when the 'Vette came by us on the left like a stealth fighter.

No vacuum. No vortex. No noise. No fanfare like the big Yellow Dragon had provided. Just strong, silent efficiency piped out through a well-tuned factory exhaust. It was plain and simple. This son of a bitch was fast. The Coupe's reign as one of the fastest hot rods on the NorCal street-racing scene was over.

WHAT REALLY MATTERED

It didn't matter that Eddie and I didn't know for sure just how much drag strip we had covered—a quarter mile, give or take a few hundred feet.

It didn't matter that we got beat by a rich kid who hadn't paid his dues with long, greasy hours in his pop's basement.

It didn't matter that his old man could afford to buy a production car off the shelf that would beat me hands down.

It didn't matter that the rich kid didn't bypass his senior prom to spend hours in the basement, readying his car for another weekend of racing.

It didn't matter that the rich kid didn't have to give up getting laid to work on his car.

It didn't matter that the rich kid didn't have to work at the gas station, study, and work on his car after school day in and day out.

What did matter was that Eddie and I did the best we could with what we had to work with.

What did matter was that the little Coupe mentored me, and gave me the self-esteem, the will to win, and the knowingness through this baptism of fire that I would need in order to launch me into the rest of my life.

What did matter was that the little Coupe bonded Eddie and me in a way that taught us how to recreate this kind of success, this juice, around some future, unknown passions that would arise again and again in our lives.

What did matter was that the little Coupe was my escape vehicle from my old man, and it allowed me to create something of my own at a time in my life when that was the most important thing for me to do.

What did matter was that my soul was deeply stirred and the fires of a relationship with God had been fanned by this initial taste for speed and the love that I felt for my little Ford coupe.

What did matter was that this rite of passage was the only one I would experience for many years in a society that was bereft of even the most infinitesimal vestige of the desperate need for an adolescent boy to make the transition into manhood.

Even if no man would tell me so, I knew I had done well.

CHAPTER 8
THE DREAM

After being discharged from the navy, I returned home and sold the Coupe. After being beat by the Duntov 'Vette, it was impossible for me to return to the good ol' days. More than a few times over the years of my flying career, I questioned my career path and wondered if I should have followed my passion for cars.

With McGill's admonition haunting me to "go back and finish school," since he had said you can't do anything without a college degree, I finished two years at City College of San Francisco and another two at San Francisco State University, completing a degree in the social sciences.

Throughout those four years, the dream of flight was gradually replacing my obsession with fast cars. I dreamt often of flying airplanes. Even though I had accumulated a few flight hours toward my private license in 1964, flying out of the old Petaluma Sky Ranch, the self-doubts still lingered.

Occasionally, McGill would come to me in dreams, and the spark of hope for a life in the air would flicker briefly but die once again upon awakening.

It wouldn't be until a strange pattern of events unfolded that I would have a clear, unobstructed path to a flying career. Over the years, I would learn to trust God that this kind of everyday miracle would unfold, if I just had the faith and patience to keep moving forward with as few expectations as possible.

A SLURRY MACHINE AND AN ANGEL

By the time I was in my mid-twenties and was a good-looking, personable kid, I'd finished college and bounced around in different jobs, sporadically accumulating twenty-five hours in my flight log book.

To make some money, I took a job selling asphalt slurry machines for a wealthy San Francisco matron. (Slurry is the overlay coat of liquid asphalt material that pavers put on top of streets to preserve the basic roadway.) She had been influenced by a friend of her recently deceased husband, who owned a paving company on the San Francisco peninsula, to purchase the distribution rights for a new type of slurry machine. He suggested she put up some of her inheritance money toward the purchase of the machine. It was built in Galion, Ohio, home to steamrollers and paving equipment of the same name.

The matron sent me to Galion for an indoctrination course on how to repair and operate the machine. Slurry machines were a far cry from flying machines, but the money was good, and I was getting my hands dirty again.

One evening, after I had been in training in Galion for a week, and after an especially long, hot day in the machine shop, I realized that this kind of work was grueling and was not how I wanted to spend the rest of my life. A wave of depression came over me for not following my dreams.

After work, still hot and sweaty, I jumped in my rental car and drove west out of Galion until I came to a roadside bar. I needed a beer to contemplate where my life was taking me.

While I was sitting at the bar, another young guy about my age sat down a couple of stools away. I struck up a conversation with him, complaining that I had made a mistake taking this job selling these Goddamn machines, and what I really wanted to do was fly airplanes.

The young man said, "Hey, man, I was just hired last week by United Airlines as a flight engineer on the DC-8. I start training in two weeks. You won't believe this, but I'd been working as a civil engineer in Cincinnati and was bored with my job.

"Then all of a sudden I come across this want ad in the paper that says: 'Wanted: Pilots for United Airlines, no flight time required!' I say to myself, *How in the hell can you be a pilot, much less a pilot for United Air Lines, without any flight time?*

"So I walk down to this hotel one Friday morning, take some tests, pass 'em, and two weeks later, I get a letter in the mail, telling me that if I want a job as a pilot for United, they'll pay for my private, commercial, and instrument ratings. And if I pass all that stuff, they'll hire me as a flight engineer on the DC-8!"

I just about choked on my beer.

"You mean you didn't have any flight time? Zip?" I asked, stunned.

"Nope, nada."

"Well, were you a flight crewmember in the military or anything? Are the other airlines hiring? How did you get the interview?"

All my self-doubts came spilling out in the form of unanswered questions to the angel, disguised as a young man, sitting next to me in this unlikely slice of heaven in the backwoods of Ohio.

"You mean, you got zero hours and they hired you?" I asked again, all the while trying to compute this incredulous possibility for myself.

DISCOVERING A WORLD OF POSSIBILITIES

I'd always assumed that all airline pilots were former military aviators, and that a flying career was unattainable for a mere enlisted mortal like myself. Plus, some part of my dream of flying died with McGill. I had put my flying dream in a box and packed it away.

The dark brown bottle of Rainier beer I held in my hand on the night I met that kid in the bar shook with the excitement of actually considering the possibility of being able to fly airplanes… and make a living doing it!

What were the odds of me sitting on a bar stool in the boondocks of Galion, Ohio, listening to this guy tell me that I could pull my own dream out of the box, dust it off, and fly away with it? This had to have been "a God thing."

When I backed the car out of the gravel parking lot in front of the bar, I looked into the review mirror and saw McGill smiling at me!

Every time I looked in the mirror as I drove slowly through the dark Ohio backwoods to the hotel, I saw McGill's easy smile.

Man, if I could pull this one off, it would be one of the biggest miracles of my life.

A SIGN

Shortly after returning from the equipment training in Ohio, I got fired from my job selling asphalt slurry machines.

I had towed the machine to Phoenix, Arizona, where I was supposed to give a slurry sealing demonstration in the parking lot of a local bank. I purposely chose a typical July day, which was hot and dry, to demo the machine, since the slurry mix needed hot temperatures to set up and seal the asphalt.

Since I had never done a live demonstration before on actual pavement, I was nervous about operating the machine's controls. Besides, after finding out about the United Airlines gig, I was far from focused on demonstrating asphalt slurry machines.

As I moved the miniature steamroller-like machine into position, I lowered the rotating slurry paddles onto the pavement and turned on the slurry flow valve.

This was all taking place near the white fence surrounding the west side of the bank's huge parking lot. Most of the bank's officers had gathered in the parking lot to see what this thing could do.

They were watching intently now, standing back alongside the white fence to the south, arms crossed in white, short-sleeved dress shirts, and ties neatly pinching their necks in the 110-degree, blazing summer heat.

At first the material didn't want to flow, so I opened the valve some more as I lowered the slurry paddles into the applicator position from the bottom of the machine.

Black, sticky asphalt slurry started flowing in front of the paddles as I put the machine in gear. But the flow was coming out way too fast for the machine's paddles to be able to lay down a smooth application of slurry.

I grabbed at the flow valve and furiously spun it closed, but not before the slurry had begun splashing out from underneath the sides of the machine.

I was rapidly approaching the fence line where the bank president's white Cadillac Coupe de Ville was parked.

My job was to lay down a windrow of slurry from a point beyond the president's car, down along the south line of fence surrounding the parking lot, and back again.

But as I approached the car, the steering controls jammed hard left. I pumped at the levers that should have applied the brakes to the right drive track of the machine, but nothing happened. The machine kept going toward the fence. I couldn't stop it or the flow of slurry, and I was on a collision course with the Cadillac.

I got the machine to stop, but not before it had passed along the right side of the Caddie and slathered black, gooey, petroleum-based sealer all over the white fence bordering the west edge of the parking lot.

It also splashed the right side of the car with the same slimy, black ooze. The stuff splashed halfway up the side of the car along its entire length. Some of it even found its way into the open passenger-side window.

The flow of slurry material was slowly oozing to a stop. To this day, I remember the image of the black sealer forming little bow waves around the bank president's wing tip shoes as he sloshed toward me through the slowly spreading pool of liquid tar pitch that surrounded the idling machine.

The bank president bore a striking resemblance to my father when he screamed at me, "Put that Goddamn thing back on the trailer, and get the hell outta here!"

As I started the machine up again, I noticed out of the corner of my eye that I had covered the big white sidewall tires on the right side of the Caddie with the black goo as well. I got fired upon returning the machine back to the office, but the whole experience was a pretty good sign that I needed to be pursuing a different career path.

BUILDING THE FOUNDATION FOR A LIFE ON THE ROAD

It was clear that it was time for a change. Nothing would deter me from pursuing my dream of flight. I would go anywhere and fly anything, if that's what it took to be in the air for the rest of my life.

I visualized myself perched in the left seat of a DC-3, cockpit window slid open and a long white silk scarf blowing back along the shiny aluminum fuselage. Africa beckoned, as did South America and the entire world.

The drive back to San Francisco from Phoenix, towing the slurry machine behind the company truck and knowing that I'd be fired upon arrival, was a very long ride. I tried to quit before she fired me, but it didn't matter. Either way, I was done.

The next day, I went down to the bank and got a loan for four thousand dollars before they found out I didn't have a job.

The following day, I went to Hertz Rent-a-Car in downtown San Francisco and got a job washing cars on the swing shift. After feeling pretty sure that I was hired (not many guys with a college degree wanted a job washing cars in those days of abundant employment opportunities), I drove down the peninsula to San Carlos Airport in my current ride, a black 1957 VW Bug, and I plunked down my money on a private, commercial, and instrument rating pilot training program at Flight Safety International. Working at Hertz would allow me to make enough money to pay my rent, be able to fly during the day, and also pay off my flying loan.

After three months of car washing, commuting to Hertz every day from Redwood City—where I rented an apartment so I could be close to San Carlos Airport—and nonstop flying, I got my private and commercial pilot's licenses and instrument rating.

After submitting applications to just about every airline I could find that was hiring, TWA hired me in September 1966 as a flight engineer with the ink still wet on my instrument-rating certificate.

I was going to be an airline pilot, with all of 180 hours in my logbook!

I was almost disappointed that I didn't get a chance to go fly DC-3s in Africa. This was the beginning of what I would call my "everyday miracles" phase.

RUNNIN' WITH THE BIG DOGS

Initial training as a flight engineer on the venerable, old Boeing 707 was tough, since I had to learn a whole new jet aircraft jargon. I sat in the same classroom with some of the men who had been my heroes in the military: aviators who had been FACs (forward air controllers) in Vietnam, Naval Academy graduates, air force jet jockeys, KC-135 pilots, marine aviators, and the like.

Here I was, questing for knowledge next to these men, preparing for an airline career just like they were. Something about my self-image was shifting, but I wasn't sure yet what it was.

During my career at TWA, I spent many more years than I had anticipated as a flight engineer, and then as a copilot as a result of the oil crisis of the seventies and the long-term effects of airline deregulation.

The oil crisis came and went, and so did my dream of rapid advancement to captain for a major airline.

I eventually made captain, twenty-three years after being promised by the airline recruiter, "Son, you'll be a captain on this property in three or four years, the way we're growin'!"

I put the icing on my dream cake by becoming a captain and instructor pilot on the McDonnell/Douglas MD-80 for the last three years of my flying career.

Twenty-three years after that chance meeting in the Ohio boondocks and my subsequent indoctrination into airline flying, I was training students who were former naval jet aviators and Annapolis graduates.

That was huge for me. I had come a long way, and I was able to see that while these men had proven themselves in military aviation by flying on and off the "boat," I was now able to sit next to and walk among them as an equal.

CHAPTER 9

THINGS, THEY ARE A-CHANGIN'

Prior to meeting Joyce, my third wife, I had volunteered for a position as a Boeing 707 first officer (copilot) at Saudi Airlines in Jeddah, Saudi Arabia, through my chief pilot's office in New York.

Saudi needed additional pilots to help fly their flights and release some of their own pilots for upgrade training to first officer and captain. Since, at that time, TWA had a contract with Saudi to help in the management of their airline operations—maintenance, line operations, flight instruction, etc.—TWA was a logical first choice for help.

Saudi Arabia is not the dating capital of the world, so when I returned home after my six-month "vacation," I was emotionally starved and thought I was ready for lasting love.

I met Joyce in Mill Valley shortly after I got back. I had been married twice before, but I thought this time it would be different. I felt more mature and ready for a different kind of experience. I had gone down to the Tamalpais High School track from my home in Homestead Valley, three blocks above the high school, for a run.

When I got there, I saw a tall, beautiful, blonde woman just rounding the last turn on the track, heading in my direction.

I started to jog, slowly enough so that she would catch up to me. When she came alongside me, I struck up a conversation with her. We talked as we jogged. She was from Wisconsin. I told her of my recent travels to Saudi Arabia. She was intrigued. I was infatuated.

The fact that I'd had two previous marriages didn't even enter into the equation with Joyce. I was unconscious of my relationship wounds and just ready to be in love, or so I thought.

One thing led to another, and we soon found ourselves in bed together.

Six months later, we were married. Two years after that, Joyce left me. I thought we had a good relationship. She did not. Her leaving me stripped away the veneer of who I thought I was. It left me without the identity of the "tough guy"—the guy who needed to prove himself with his accomplishments, his running, his accumulation of advanced degrees—that I had spent my whole life unconsciously constructing. I thought I had lost the only woman I'd ever loved, but I was clueless as to what real love was.

My wife leaving me initiated my breakthrough to being able to feel my emotions. This beginning of feeling would eventually lead to my heart opening to God, to others and, most important, myself. This was truly the beginning of my spiritual life.

When I look back on it, I know it was the turning point of my life; without it, I would not have been able to begin the "surrender" process to God the way I was being forced to then.

For the next twenty years, God began to slowly change me. He would reveal my strength as a leader of men; as a compassionate, open-hearted man; and as a man whose word could be counted on.

I took some time off after Joyce left me and fell into a daily pattern of crying and feeling sorry for myself. I listened to music at all hours, which helped to purge long-held feelings of sadness and fear while, at the same time, connecting me to a rhythm that I had never felt before. I voraciously read anything that smacked of spiritual philosophy. I walked a daily circuit of aimless wanderings through the bookstore and forest trails around my home in Mill Valley.

I craved music. I spent hours lying on the living room floor of my home listening to all kinds of music, but mostly to music that reverberated loose the sadness and grief that I had covered up for so long.

I spent $800 on a sound system for my little VW Rabbit. This would ensure that there would be no gaps, from home to wherever else, in the rhythms and sounds that I found myself suddenly craving.

I played the album *Jonathan Livingston Seagull* by the hour, crying endlessly, and was moved by the power of the words of my brother aviators, Richard Bach and his friend Jonathan.

Through Jonathan's words, I felt a kinship with all aviators, as well as with my fellow travelers. I was awed by the way in which Jonathan was transmuted through Richard and was gifted to humanity.

The album was made even more powerful by the narration of the rich, melodious voice of young Richard Harris, the British actor who would stun me later with his portrayal of a Lakota Sioux Sun Dancer in *A Man Called Horse*.

After two months of this immersion, I was ready for some baby steps back into a world that had become foreign to me; it now moved too fast, sounded too harsh, seemed too crass, and felt too violent. I was now somehow different, more vulnerable, and yet more resilient.

THE RESURRECTION

During my leave from flying, I was literally grounded by the pain of the loss of Joyce. For the first time ever, I couldn't run away from the pain. I couldn't deny it. I was now forced to just feel whatever feelings were surfacing. It was the first time I could remember feeling anything. With every step I took in this pain, I felt rooted to the earth and strangely grateful for the pain's slowing effect on me.

I ventured out of the house only to shop, to eat an occasional meal out, and to meander slowly down to the old Mill Valley train depot/bookstore, where I would numbly scan the shelves for whatever written word might appear to help me in my healing process.

During these outings, I began to see and hear things I had never seen and heard before: small birds flying here and there, making their nests, and playing with each other amidst their daily chores; the vibrant colors that all of a sudden now surrounded me, forced me to stop in my tracks, so newly imprinted was I with the force of nature's majestic splendor; little children who, in their laughing and playing, reminded me painfully of my loneliness growing up in the wind and fog of San Francisco.

This new ability to slow down, to feel things that I had formerly considered too painful, was eye-opening. I had a new awareness of my place in God's universe, and this new identity as a man who should be loved just as himself, without "qualifying," would become a touchstone for everything I would do.

I would at times fall back into my old habits of moving too fast, too impulsively, but the feeling that resulted from this regression would be too painful to ignore.

SPIRITUAL MATERIALISM

During my time as a pilot with TWA, I had become casual friends with an airline couple, Ken and Kathleen. My judgment of Ken was not unlike my judgments of most other pilots I knew at that time. I found most of my cockpit buddies friendly enough, but there were very few of them that I felt a spiritual kinship to.

Many of them, externally, seemed to lack heart and imagination. Too many of them seemed to be in denial about their need for some kind of a spiritual philosophy of life. This was during the beginning of my arrogant "better than the rest of you pilots because I'm a spiritual guy" phase.

I recognize now that my arrogance was a psychological backlash, the result of my not wanting to own that same part of myself that was heartless, closed down, and unimaginative.

It was that part of me that didn't feel good enough amongst my former heroes rearing its ugly head again. It caused me to bolster myself with my self-perceived spiritual superiority.

After I recovered enough from losing Joyce to begin thinking about my life and how I couldn't continue to live like I had been, I signed up for a six-month psychological healing program called Psychospiritual Integration (PSI). That program helped me to take a look at those parts of me that I had denied or repressed. It also began to reveal some deeply buried character flaws that I needed to rethink.

After the class, I thought I had something to hang my hat on that I felt better than them about. I was able to one-up them with my obviously heightened awareness of life beyond flying.

I could easily justify spiritual pride since, in my own mind, I couldn't measure up to their superior intelligence, flying skill, and overall heroic stature. As a result of PSI, I now considered myself a "spiritual seeker." So I had stumbled upon this unknown version of my spiritual self, something I judged most of them knew little about and were possibly afraid of.

I wore it as a mantle that kept me separate from and better than others, in my own mind. The possibility that I might not be as intelligent as others was too painful to consider and admit to, so I covered my feelings of inferiority with a holier-than-thou attitude.

I use the term "spiritual materialism" to describe this behavior. It's similar to the behavior exhibited by people who consider themselves religious because they go to church on Sunday, while the rest of the week they justify their less-than-spiritual behavior.

I carried the wounds of a little boy who never felt good enough so deeply that I would unconsciously do anything to elevate myself in comparison to the other men I had placed myself in the midst of.

I would eventually learn to love myself enough, so I could feel the love for and enjoy the camaraderie of other men who'd once threatened me. It became clear that it was not my job to compete with or be better than them, but to discover and utilize my own unique gifts in service to others.

The absolute perfection of the scenario I found myself in was that I had picked a career in which I was mostly surrounded by bright, accomplished, former-military officers, which was so much the better because they continued to highlight my shortcomings and force me to work on myself.

It was becoming obvious that I couldn't have picked a better career to usher me onto the path of personal healing that I needed to follow to move into the next phase of my life's work.

CHAPTER 10
GURU TIME

After completing my meanderings through Mill Valley, I often ate lunch at one of my favorite quasi-health-food restaurants, Good Earth in Larkspur Landing.

One day, while approaching the front door of the restaurant, I ran into Ken and Kathleen. We sat down for lunch and talked about flying and what was going on in our lives. As we talked, I realized I was feeling uplifted and connected to something besides my pain for the first time since my separation and subsequent divorce. I was hopeful about this new direction my life was beginning to take as we chattered enthusiastically.

I told Kathleen about an article I had read in a recent issue of the *Yoga Journal*. The article described the writer's experience during her visit with an Indian teacher at his ashram in the foothills of the Himalayas. He was a guru and teacher to many others. I had never considered myself the type of guy who needed a guru, but something about the article touched me, and I knew I had to go to India.

Kathleen and I agreed that a trip to India would not only be fun but would also be in our spiritual best interests. We finished our three-hour lunch with a firm promise to check in with one another in the next week. Ken seemed to be tolerantly amused at our spiritual seeking. We asked him to go with us, but he declined.

Kathleen said she would see if Audrey, a mutual friend and massage therapist, would want to go as well. Audrey and Kathleen had known each other for some time, and Kathleen knew that Audrey would be open to accompanying her. It would turn out that both Kathleen and Audrey wanted to visit another Indian guru, in a different part of India. This worked out well, since they could accompany me to my guru's ashram, spend a week there, and then trek to another part of India to visit their guru, Sathya Sai Baba.

THE JOURNEY HEATS UP

The following week, I called Kathleen. Not only had her friend agreed to accompany us, but she'd already checked into air travel to India. Our little band of spiritual seekers was assembled and ready to go.

Kathleen and I obtained interline passes (free passes for airline employees) on Swiss Air to Frankfurt, and then on Air India to New Delhi. Audrey would fly on TWA interline "friend" passes provided for her by Kathleen.

I wrote to the Indian guru that had been featured in the magazine and asked permission for us to stay at his ashram during our time in India.

The ashram was located in the Kumaon Hills of the Nainital district of Uttar Pradesh, India, a seven-hour cab ride northeast from New Delhi. The guru, Babaji, welcomed most people to visit the ashram, free of charge. Our only commitment was to work in the ashram, cleaning, painting, and doing other odd jobs while we absorbed the daily spiritual blessings from the guru.

We received permission by way of a letter dated August 8, 1980, to come to Herakhan, the nearest village to the ashram, during our planned trip there in November. A messenger from the ashram would meet us in the little village of Herakhan once we arrived there via taxi from New Delhi. He would contact us when we arrived in the village. We figured it wouldn't be too hard for him to find us since we would probably be the only Americans in town.

Underlying my search for a spiritual teacher was a need to continue the apprenticeship in manhood that McGill had begun. Besides my Uncle Pete, I had never known a man I could learn from or look up to. It would become clear to me later that I was looking for more affirmation from men in authority and leadership positions, and I received that from Babaji.

I wasn't aware yet of my being on a spiritual search. I just knew that my life wasn't working. I was being offered this time to discover a deeper purpose in life, beyond my flying career. I was content to follow whatever presented itself to me, which was unusual behavior for a man who formerly needed to be in control of his life.

INDIA, THE SPIRITUAL MATRIX

Herakhan Baba, also known as Babaji, was a well-known and respected Indian guru, who was considered a saint in India for his selfless service and teachings of a path to enlightenment. (The name Baba in India means elder or teacher; the title "ji" is tacked onto the end of the names of many Indian elders and teachers as a symbol of respect.)

Since Kathleen was not what you would consider an outdoorsy type, we—Ken, Kathleen, and I—felt it was necessary to prepare for our India trip by taking Kathleen on a "shakedown" backpacking trip into the Sierra Nevada mountains, south of Lake Tahoe in California, so she could experience "roughing it."

This was for the sole purpose of indoctrinating her into life in a developing country, sans toilet paper, or sans anything resembling Western toilets for that matter, since her idea of "roughing it," up to that point, was staying at a Days Inn and ordering room service.

She was not looking forward to being without her makeup, special health food, and manicurist. Audrey, on the other hand, was comfortable in the outdoors, so she chose to forgo the Tahoe trip.

The trip went well. We "roughed" it by packing three gallons of packaged wine into the backcountry. We spent the first night around the campfire, enjoying the wine so we wouldn't have to carry any of it back out with us. Kathleen turned out to be a much better outdoorswoman than we suspected. This talent would come in handy on our return trip from India, when she would care for Audrey and me when we got sick in Athens, Greece. We had to stay in a hotel for two days before resuming our trip back to the States.

A CUP OF CULTURE SHOCK

After our flight from London to New Delhi, Kathleen, Audrey, and I decompressed for two days in the New Delhi Hyatt Hotel. After walking around the city and being bombarded by the strange sights, smells, sounds, and the hundreds of vendors who offered to do everything from shine our shoes to massage us to book us into their hotel, all simultaneously, we decided it was time to get on with what we came to do.

We hired a cab to drive us from New Delhi to the little village of Haldwani, the jumping-off point for the trek upriver to Herakhan. The cab ride was a seven-hour trip into the foothills of the Himalayas. It was hot, dusty, and uneventful, except for one incident.

During the ride across the belly of India, we stopped at a railroad crossing to wait for a local train to cross the road. It looked like a long wait, so the Indian cab driver turned the ignition off, and we all got out of the cab to stretch and relieve ourselves.

Part of the aforementioned Sierra Nevada shakedown trip was to outfit Kathleen with a "pee cup." It has a small, funnel-like protrusion on the front of the cup that allows women to pee standing up.

After we climbed out of the cab, I went over to the side of the road and walked under a tree to relieve myself; Kathleen followed me. This in itself got the cab driver's attention. He happened to look over his right shoulder from his position alongside the left front fender of the taxi, an old, four-door '61 Chevy. He was smoking a cigarette and watching the train roll by.

I unzipped, and so did Kathleen. As I peed, so did she. The driver's mouth dropped open. His cigarette seemed to hang in midair as it dropped from his hand to the ground. He absent-mindedly stabbed at it with his foot, attempting to stamp it out. He missed it by a foot in either direction. He was fixated on Kathleen.

As the last of the railroad cars passed the intersection, I zipped up. Kathleen hesitated an instant longer, shaking her little hose to drip dry for additional effect. Then she zipped up. We sauntered back to the cab.

The driver gave both of us a wide berth, but he continued to stare at Kathleen. We climbed back in the cab, the three of us in the back seat as before. For the next four hours of the journey to Haldwani, the driver shifted his eyes constantly from the road to the rearview mirror and back again, so much so that I was afraid we were going to get in an accident.

I was tempted to buy one of those devices and send it to the driver back in India with an explanation of what it was used for, but I never did. I figured the meaning would have been lost in the translation.

THE GURU AS MENTOR

We pulled into Haldwani on November 11, 1980. This little village served as the spiritual base camp for seekers en route to Babaji's ashram up the Gatham Ganga River to the village of Herakhan. The driver took us to the Kailash Hotel, where we would stay for two nights before continuing our trek to Herakhan.

I found out later, we got ripped off for 900 rupees (about $120) for the ride from New Delhi to Haldwani. It was cheap by American standards, but should have cost much less.

The exorbitant price, by Indian standards, was confirmed by some of the local ashram people. For whatever good it would do, I made a mental note to tell Babaji about the inflated cab price in the hope he could warn other visiting seekers of this practice.

It was eleven months after my forty-first birthday and I was right on target for my midlife crisis.

LEARNING TO TRUST THE PROCESS

We checked out of the Kailash Hotel on November 13, after continuing to "decompress" from our long cab ride across India and our flight from the United States.

Kathleen, Audrey, and I were standing around outside the hotel, kibitzing about the greasy food, the rats in the toilet, and the bedbugs. We were also trying to figure out how we would find the person who was going to take us to the ashram, when a little Indian man in a yellow burlap suit and a pointed yellow hat suddenly appeared from around the corner of the red brick foundation of the hotel.

"Are you de people from America going to de Babaji ashram?" he said in that strangely indecisive, endearingly lilting, head-waggling Indian mannerism. "Come with me. I vill take you to de ashram."

After checking it out with each other and figuring that we were being watched over by someone higher up than us, the man told us to gather up our luggage.

"I vill meet you in front of de hotel in vun hour, please."

He pulled up in the dirtiest, faded olive-drab, vintage, seventies Land Rover I had ever seen. The driver picked up our luggage, helped us into the Land Rover, and drove us to a place called Damsite where he dropped us off and another man met us. He was to be our guide upriver to Babaji's ashram.

By now, we had picked up a young couple: a nice but naïve, and (we would discover later) very promiscuous, young Dutch girl and her boyfriend.

THE MONKEY GOD WELCOMES

After crossing the river some six times on our eight-kilometer walk down the meandering, mostly dry Gautam Ganga River, the head waters of the holy river Ganges, we rounded the final bend.

I was in the lead and had just finished adjusting the shoulder straps on my backpack and scrunching it into a new position.

I looked up and saw a large red statue of a monkey, perched on a huge boulder in the riverbed off to my left. It was the Hindu Monkey

God, Hanuman. (Hanuman was the mighty ape that aided Lord Rama in his expedition against evil forces and is one of the most popular idols in the Hindu pantheon.)

Some thirty yards upstream from the statue, on the same side of the river, was the dark cave where Babaji was said to have mysteriously appeared in 1970. He was discovered there, so the legend goes, by a Herakhan farmer named Chandramani. The farmer was so impressed by the boy's radiance, beauty, and power that he began serving him.

Shortly thereafter, they climbed the holy mountain behind the cave, Mt. Kailash, where the boy sat in a perfectly still yogic posture for forty-five days, neither eating nor drinking nor opening his eyes.

Later, he and Chandramani crossed the river to the small village of Herakhan to live in a small hut. One by one, awestruck villagers came to pay their respects to this remarkable young man, believing him to be the Herakhan Baba of prior incarnations.

THE ASHRAM

My eyes swept across the river and caught the bright white paint on the 108 stairs leading up the steep riverbank across from the monkey statue. The freshly painted white stairs that led up to the ashram stood out in sharp contrast to the brown dirt of the riverbank. The steps had to be painted yearly, since most of them were underwater during the monsoon season.

Coming upon this statue so suddenly, and in this unlikely place, brought me a strange feeling of peace, of coming home amidst the incongruity—the seven-hour cab ride, the twelve-thousand mile flight, numerous airports, and four days of travel.

I felt deeply connected to the thousands of spiritual pilgrims who must have been drawn to, comforted by, and inspired by this archetypal icon in their own journeys over the centuries.

MY SPIRITUAL ROOTS

Nothing in my Catholic upbringing prepared me for what I was about to experience. Even though I poke fun at the skill with which the Catholic

Church has elevated guilt to an art form, and though I sometimes take shadowy, fiendish delight in reading about the current dysfunctional sexual antics exhibited by some Catholic priests, I owe much of my spiritual foundation to my upbringing in the Catholic Church.

Because of the church's influence, however, I began a gradual down-hill slide from being an altar boy of questionable devotion, to being groomed for possible entry into the priesthood, to being spiritually comatose for the better part of the next thirty years.

VERY PRACTICAL SPIRITUALITY

Prior to my now unquenchable thirst for truth and spiritual knowl-edge, the most religious fervor I could muster consisted of two things I'd done faithfully as a squadron crewmember on board the USS *Randolph*: taking the sacrament of communion while attending daily mass onboard ship, and practicing holding my breath every day for as long as I could.

I attended daily mass and communion because I wanted to be in a "state of grace" (a prerequisite for going to Catholic heaven—a worthy goal in itself, and one of the basic tenets of the Catholic faith) if the aircraft in which I was flying got a "dead cat shot." (A dead cat shot is when the catapult, the steam- or hydraulic-pressured mechanical slingshot that flung the aircraft off the carrier deck, suddenly loses pressure and weakly spits the aircraft into the water ahead of the steaming carrier with insufficient flying speed to remain airborne.)

After mass and before flying, I practiced holding my breath for as long as I could for the same reason, in the event the aircraft I was flying in went into the water and I needed to be able to hold my breath for a long period of time.

I was looking for something that was real, something that wouldn't accuse me of committing a mortal sin or tell me I was destined to spend an eternity in Hell if I missed Sunday mass or ate meat on Friday.

I was looking for something that would celebrate my "original blessing," as Matthew Fox writes of, instead of the concept of original sin—something I could practice more often than on Sundays, without wearing stuffy clothes, and without having to enter a large, hideously decorated, expensive building with lots of plaster statues peering at me from every corner.

WHAT METHOD WAS THERE TO MY MADNESS?

After cresting the 108 steps leading up to the ashram from the river, we stepped into a large courtyard that was surrounded by big concrete planter boxes, which contained a cornucopia of tropical trees, plants, and flowers.

We were immediately enveloped in the luscious fragrance of this domestic jungle, which was interlaced by meandering walkways that led to an arch at the end of the courtyard. In addition to its being the gateway to the courtyard temple, it acted as a trellis for more beautiful climbing flowers and vines.

This visual display was accompanied by a potpourri of smells, which blended together into what I can now only describe as a powerful, aromatic, therapeutic mix.

Interspersed throughout the garden were Hindu statues, bells, and a mix of devotional paraphernalia that was foreign to me, but which

I would become familiar with over the next few weeks as I allowed myself to embrace the spirituality of this most gracious host.

In my fear, I was eagerly willing to trade the stifling familiarity of the Catholic Church for these strange surroundings.

I silently reminded myself to trust the process that brought me here. This was strange territory, since I usually had a plan for everything. But for the first time, my heart was leading the way, and its plan was not to be so easily defined.

We were greeted immediately by a beautiful, dark-skinned young woman in an Indian sari. It was Gora Devi, the same young Italian woman who served as Babaji's Girl Friday and who had typed my invitation to visit the ashram from Babaji back in August.

Even though this place looked strange and I thought everybody was smiling too much, I felt an openness, a welcome that belied the strange surroundings.

I, too, would learn the transformative power of joy without any good reason and how to perform "random acts of kindness and senseless acts of beauty." It would be some time before I would learn to smile for no good reason, though. To this day, I still have trouble doing this.

It was here that I would also learn the power of apparently doing nothing, of playing in spite of my never having been taught how, and of releasing my fear of looking silly while doing so. It was here that I would have insights into the direction for my life and tap into my internal guidance systems through "creative hanging out" with no apparent purpose.

This apparent purposelessness would fly in the face of everything I had been raised to believe, even though it worked for my parents' generation, God bless them.

"Work hard, save your money, don't waste time, don't be silly, act your age." These were the lessons I'd learned growing up.

These were all recommendations that I had now been forced to confront, and to acknowledge how deeply I had bought into them, while respecting the time capsule they had been conceived in. It was time for me to move beyond them.

CLASS BEGINS

I could not afford to be suspicious in this place. I didn't travel halfway around the world to miss out on the love, healing, and spiritual mentoring that I so desperately sought.

Since Babaji would shortly be conducting his daily informal afternoon *sadhana*, his spiritual teaching, we followed Gora Devi hurriedly to our humble little orange huts where the visiting devotees slept.

The Dutch girl and her boyfriend had been caught making love on the cool stone floor of one of these little huts. I honored them for taking the risk to consecrate their arrival here. But risks carry consequences, and they were ushered out of the ashram and back down the riverbed from whence they came.

My imagination of her lying naked on the stone floor with her boyfriend on top of her stirred my sexual juices, and with that came a strange fear and incongruity of having those feelings in this holy place. If the guru was as clairvoyant as described, he could just as easily throw me out of the ashram for my lurid thoughts.

We dropped our backpacks on the floor and reassembled in the courtyard, along with the rest of the ashram's guests who, parting the leaves and flowers like so many native hunters emerging from the jungle, silently emerged into the courtyard from all directions.

We took our place on cushions that had been placed on the concrete floor of the courtyard, joining the semicircle formed by the other guests around Babaji. He sat cross-legged on the courtyard floor, gently sniffing a few of his favorite flowers, his back supported by the wall that snaked its way through the courtyard.

A SPIRITUAL MENTOR

Although I was skeptical as I sat down in front of this spiritual anomaly, what kept me grounded and somehow able to integrate this experience into my limited worldview was the fact that I saw this teacher as a man, first and foremost.

I'm sure he had feet of clay, as does every man, although I never saw that side of him while at the ashram. He had his human frailties, but as a holy man, he was capable of performing acts that defied logical description, such as supposedly appearing in two different places at once, to two different people, lightening his body by making it less dense to allow myself and another devotee of the ashram to carry him up a steep hill with no effort.

In my mind, I tried to rank him with the holiest of men that I knew of, Jesus Christ. Since I was attempting to compare this man before me with a man who walked the earth two thousand years ago, and whom I had known only through my religious upbringing and infinitesimal faith, the mystique and inaccessible mythical stature surrounding Jesus placed Him in a league beyond Babaji.

It would become apparent to me years later that there was no comparison between Babaji and Jesus; Jesus would show up in my life in a way that left no doubt in my mind that He was the alpha and the omega, "the way, the truth, and the life" for me.

At the time, I considered the possibility of replacing Jesus with Babaji, since the Catholic Church seemed to offer me no reason not to. The temptation to adopt wholesale another culture's religion that embraced what my early Catholicism overlooked was great. It offered me a spiritual teacher in the flesh to learn from rather than a statue representing an omnipresent God to kneel before and pray to. My faith was no longer, if it ever had been, strong enough. I needed a sign.

I needed to touch and be touched by, to talk to and be listened to, and to be accepted by a man of Babaji's stature before I could accept others. This man had something for me that the other men in my life, aside from my Uncle Pete and McGill, hadn't been able to give me.

ROLLED IN GOLD

Before I could open my heart to myself and others, before I could access the gifts that lay dormant in my soul, before I could get on with being who it was I was created to be, I needed to be accepted and loved for just who I was, with no conditions, no expectations, without having to "do it right," without having to grovel for it.

I was here to learn what this man could teach me about opening my heart, to unlock the love that I knew that I had to give, first to myself and then to others, to learn to serve through discovering my unique gifts.

And yet, I was not willing to hand my life over to this man. Babaji would chastise me for not unquestioningly obeying him as so many of his European devotees did. Their ability to submit their will to his higher purpose far exceeded anything I was willing or capable of doing at the time.

Later, when I read what Joseph Campbell writes about gurus in *The Open Life*, I exonerated myself:

I think the guru can be a delusion... The thing about the guru in the West is that he represents an alien principle of the spirit, namely, that you don't follow your own path; you follow a given path. And that's totally contrary to the Western spirit! Our spirituality is of the individual quest, individual realization—authenticity in your life out of your own center. So you must take the message from the East, assimilate it to your own dimension and to your own thrust of life, and not get pulled off track.

Babaji did teach me in a way that I could grasp and that worked for me, but not in the way I might have expected. He made me aware of my arrogance and my need for humility by reflecting my ego back to me on many occasions. He tested me by making me "special" in the ashram, allowing me to accompany him on his strolls through the ashram grounds, taking rupees from me to give to the villagers who tended the gardens and staffed the ashram, thereby seeing how I would respond to this "chosen" status.

As I would later discover, the work I was doing with this man in a small village in the Himalayan foothills was a harbinger of my heart's work to come.

I now know that the Italian altar boy that was chosen for the priesthood was fulfilling that prophecy in his own way. That vocation was manifesting full-circle in an altogether different form that I could never have imagined.

When I was ready to return to the States, I inquired of Babaji as to how I might better serve mankind after having spent this time with him.

I must have passed the ashram tests because he said to me, "Go home, Filot [my nickname, since he chose not to pronounce Pilot correctly], and practice love, simplicity, and truth."

And my response was, "Yes, Babaji, I know that, but what more can I do?" As if there were anything more to do than practice love, simplicity, and truth!

His final response was, "Go home, Filot, practice love, simplicity, and truth. You have been rolled in gold."

CHAPTER 11
THE BEGINNING OF "NORMAL, EVERYDAY MIRACLES"

After returning home from India, something shifted in me. Among other changes that would later manifest, I had a deep realization that I had been a "taker" for most of my life. I was selfish, narcissistic, and only concerned about myself.

The India journey was the first time I consciously left behind the world I had been racing through. The vastly different Indian culture—the smells, the sights, the sounds, and the tight family connections among the people in the villages I visited—helped me face the sadness and loneliness of how disconnected I was from the people around me: my friends, my family, my former wives, my crewmembers.

I began to feel the pain of how I had hurt the women I had been with up to that point, how I had disregarded them in running roughshod over their feelings with my single-minded selfishness.

I felt the pain of being so disconnected from the love I so dearly wanted and needed, and I knew that I couldn't live like this any longer.

After settling back into the Bay Area, I resumed my voracious reading of anything spiritual. During that time, I heard about a graduate school in the East Bay, John F. Kennedy University, that offered a three-year Master's degree in Transpersonal Counseling Psychology. Something about the transpersonal (beyond the personal, essentially spiritual counseling) sounded like a way I could follow up on the spiritual path that led me to India. I had been deeply affected by the culture and people of India, enough so that I wanted to retain something of its beauty and deep spiritual essence in my new life back home.

The transpersonal curriculum had enough esoteric Eastern philosophy and comparative religion studies to satisfy my new thirst for the kind of spirituality that seemed to be in such short supply here in the U.S.

Combined with the Eastern studies would be the required counseling courses that I would need in order to sit for most any state board exams for licensing as a Professional Counselor or Marriage and Family Therapist.

As it turned out, part of the requirement for completion of my Master's degree was ongoing psychotherapy sessions with a licensed psychologist or psychotherapist, who would help me work on my newly surfacing "issues."

This new path felt like a way that I could pay back some of what I felt I had taken from my world.

As a result of my time at the ashram and my exposure to Hindu culture, I had developed an interest in the other Eastern religions as well—Buddhism, Islam, Taoism, and others.

These religions gave me an expanded perspective on spirituality that was missing in the Catholicism of my youth.

When I returned from India, I resumed my flying job as a pilot for TWA. When I thought about how I would attend class full-time, write papers, and do everything else that a graduate student was supposed to do, I couldn't imagine how I would pull this off and fly a full schedule for my airline.

I was also painfully aware that, at age forty-one, I would be "the old guy" in a class full of twenty- and thirty-somethings.

It was during this time, the early '80s, that TWA was going through big changes. Pilot advancement was stagnant, and many of the pilots were being furloughed. Many of them were also being bumped back, in my case, from copilot to flight engineer on the Lockheed L1011.

I had been a junior copilot, near the bottom of the seniority list on the Lockheed. So when I got bumped back to flight engineer, that placed me near the top of the flight-engineer seniority list since each pilot category—captain, copilot, and flight engineer—had its own separate seniority list.

That meant I could have a shot at some pretty choice trips as a senior flight engineer and could avoid the "red eye" and "freight dog" cargo flights.

This also meant that I could bid as a "reserve" pilot and not have to fly as often as I would have if I had held "a line of time." A line of time was a series of regularly scheduled flights that pilots bid for, and when awarded, were obligated to fly during any particular month. A typical line of time required pilots to be gone at least half the month. Not good for a serious graduate student. I was learning, however, to "trust the process" as a result of some significant shifts in my perspective.

So I signed on at JFK and started classes. During my three years there, I met some inspired and inspiring young students that became my school "family."

But as a professional nomad and now spiritual seeker with unlimited free airline travel passes, I felt the need to deepen and continue my search for God knew what.

"TAKE A PARANORMAL JOURNEY..."

It was during the middle of my first year at JFK that I felt the need to continue my search. I had taken one of my leaves of absence from TWA, and I was on top of my coursework in school, so I had the travel time I needed.

It was May, one of the hottest months in the Philippines, in 1981 when I chose to fly to Manila. My trip came about as a result of my relationship with a young couple, David and Jenny, whom I had met in San Rafael, California.

I had experienced some of their healing work and was impressed with who they were as people and the results they were getting with their clients.

They had studied with a teacher in the Philippines, a faith healer who had a major influence on their work as hands-on faith healers in Marin County.

Even though I didn't consider myself a hands-on healer, there was something I needed to know about faith healers that would help my work in the future. What I witnessed in Jenny and David told me that I needed to go to Manila to learn from and experience their teacher's work. It made no logical sense to travel halfway around the world on a hunch, but I was getting better at trusting my gut.

It would become clear to me some years later that what I really went to the Philippines for was to begin to trust more of my right-brain thinking, the kind that is visual and artistic and that processes information in an intuitive and simultaneous way, looking first at the whole picture and then the details.

In some ways, I felt like I was paying Uncle Pete, McGill, and Babaji back for their mentorship by readying myself to be an agent for God.

So that's how I found myself hunkered down in row thirty-four of the coach section of a Philippine Airlines 747, bound for Honolulu, and then Manila. Having learned the tricks of the airline employee trade as a "magic carpet" pass rider, I asked the agent to seat me in an empty row if possible.

My wish was granted. Now I had more than enough time, since the flight was five hours to Honolulu and another eight hours from Honolulu to Manila, and enough space to stretch out and look over the notes I had received from David and Jenny in preparation for my Philippine pilgrimage.

I also had the phone number of David and Jenny's teacher to call once I landed in Manila.

After checking into the Manila Hilton and decompressing from jet lag for a couple of days, I experienced a deep sense of loneliness that was strangely laced with excitement and hope. I walked around town aimlessly, unable to relax into a normal "tourist" mode.

I decided it was time to get what I came for, so, after checking out of the hotel, I hopped a bus for a four-hour ride to the little town of Carmen in the province of Pangasanan.

When I arrived in Carmen, I hired a motorized tricycle to take me to the little village of Rosales, home of Paz Navalta, a Filipino healer and David and Jenny's teacher.

A LADY MENTOR

I climbed out of the little single-seat, open-sided rickshaw cab covered by a faded blue awning and powered by some kind of two-stroke motorcycle engine that had long since blown its power out the tiny, disintegrating exhaust pipe in stringy clouds of acrid blue smoke.

I wiped the sweat off my forehead with the back of my hand and reached into my fanny pack for the five pesos fare. I found out later from Paz that the ride was supposed to cost only one peso.

I was greeted on the main road by Paz, one of her dogs, and her two little children. She asked me, in a mixture of Tagalog, the native Filipino language, and broken English, to come into the house.

The modest, open-screen-sided, white house was set down an inlaid-rock walkway with chickens and dogs and cats and ducks running, squawking, cackling, and barking everywhere.

As soon as we got in the door, Paz headed for the kitchen and started fixing me some lunch. I ate while she and the kids and the dog watched me. When I was through eating, she showed me to my room upstairs.

It was a plain bedroom, with a chest of drawers at the foot of the bed along one wall and a four-poster double bed with posts extending about five feet above the mattress. An enormous mosquito net was hung from the posts and draped down over the entire bed. The bottom of the netting extended down along the sides of the bed by two feet or so, almost to the floor.

The room had a view of the vegetable and flower garden, which was surrounded by a large, white brick wall.

Sweat was pouring out of me, while Paz and the kids looked cool and composed. I had no idea my body held so much water. For the next two days, my favorite pastime was lying under the mosquito netting, sweating, in a semi-comatose state, and looking heavenward for a sign that this journey would somehow provide me with some answers to my life's purpose.

Instead, what I got was an elaborate reptilian high-wire act being played out by a crack team of large geckos working five feet above my head. All I could think of was that one of them would lose the suction on their feet or miss a pass from one trapeze to another and plummet into my netting when their death-defying act went awry.

I awoke before sunup on the second day and, as I thought I was sufficiently acclimated to the 90-percent-plus humidity, got up and went out for a five-mile run.

After about two miles, I ground to a halt, overcome by the humidity. I knew this was not a good idea and started walking back to the house. This latest challenge convinced me that I was not here for a vacation. I was here to do some serious work, though I didn't yet know what that was.

As I walked back through the streets that were now awake with the local people walking to work and opening shops, I looked skyward as I heard the roar of an aircraft pass low overhead.

It was an Air Force C-130 cargo plane on final approach to some jungle air base. I immediately thought that my exit strategy out of this steam bath might be to follow the flight path of the aircraft to the base, and head for the cool ambiance of the officers' club and an ice-cold Dos Equis.

Nah. Again, I didn't come all this way to wimp out on what God might have in store for me. I couldn't have guessed what was soon to happen.

The second night at Paz's, she fixed me a wonderful dinner of fresh fish, white rice, beans, fresh salad picked from the garden, and Tang, their favorite drink. She and the kids watched my every move.

"You need to be strong for what is ahead," Paz said to me.

"Thank you, Paz. You and your family are being so kind to me. Is there anything I can do to repay you?" I asked her.

"The only thing you must do is keep your heart open and fully receive what is coming, so that you can help to heal others when you return home. You will be doing good things with men who are in great need of healing." This was the first indication of what I was really there for.

The whole scene in this remote village beside the Philippine jungle, searching for God only knows, moving from strange place to another strange place, meeting the people who unquestioningly accepted my presence there, was very surreal. Many times a day, I would wonder if I was on a wild goose chase. The comfort and affluence of Marin County was light years away.

More than once, I wondered why I wasn't home enjoying myself, finding a new woman, riding my motorcycle, or just hanging with friends.

But at the same time, I felt my heart swell with gratitude and love for these people who opened their home to me, a complete stranger. This feeling of gratitude was new to me. Up till now, I hadn't stopped long enough to feel anything, much less gratitude. I would later discover that this feeling of gratitude was helping to open the rusty gates of my heart.

MY FRIEND, JESUS

After dinner, Paz went into the other room and brought out a Bible, handed it to me, and asked me to read some passages, one of which was II Corinthians, chapter 5, verses 16–17: "So from now on we regard no one from a worldly point of view. Though we once regarded Christ in this way, we do so no longer. Therefore, if anyone is in Christ, he is a new creation; the old has gone, the new has come!"

I hadn't picked up a Bible since I attended mandatory catechism classes as a seven-year-old kid at St. Finn Barr's, my local Catholic church back in San Francisco. She told me to read the passages and then to meditate on how a given passage might apply to me. It would be years before I would venture back to Scripture for answers to the questions of my life.

After I finished my meditation, Paz went into a trance and proceeded to give me general answers to most of the questions that I had.

Questions like: What will my life's work be? When will I realize what it is, and when will I truly pursue it? Where will I live? Will I find fulfillment in this life? And one that popped out of my mouth without me even realizing it: How long will I fly for my airline?

Up to that point, I just assumed that I would fly until I was sixty, the mandatory retirement age for commercial pilots at that time, then retire and fade gracefully but unconsciously into the sunset of my life.

The questions that she couldn't answer she said would be answered when I left the Philippines. She appeared to be talking to me in a normal way, but the entire time it was clear that she was in a trance.

She told me again, "You will be doing some important healing work with men."

Then she gave me some words to use when the time came to help others with their healing. She asked me to hold my hands together in front of my face and look into my open palms.

After doing this for a few minutes with my eyes partially closed, she asked me what I saw.

"I saw the face of Jesus!" I told her.

She said that no one else that she had worked with had seen the face of Jesus. She said that I was clairvoyant.

"Right…" was my skeptical response.

Even though I was skeptical, seeing the face of Jesus here in the Philippines, thousands of miles away from home, incongruous as it was, gave me a glimmer of hope that my newly awakening spiritual nature was being affirmed.

Shortly after this, she told me, "Mister Bert, go up to your room and rest because we are going to church later this evening."

I thought this was rather strange, church late in the evening. But I was here to learn, and that meant that I needed to put my agenda aside and open myself to the possibility that God had something else in store for me.

JUST ANOTHER NIGHT IN THE JUNGLE WITH GOD

Some time later, on Thursday, May 21, 1981, I had slept lousy the night before because the mosquitoes had made multiple raids on my hopelessly penetrable netting defense system.

I felt surprisingly good nonetheless. I must have been getting acclimated to the heat, since I went out for a six-mile run at 5:00 AM and actually completed it, although I got curious stares from the local villagers.

On my run, I noticed that the people grew crops in the riverbeds during the dry season, utilizing all the available land for production and reaping the benefit of the last monsoon's silting.

Paz had breakfast ready for me when I returned from my run: scrambled eggs, fresh tomatoes from the garden, potatoes, and Tang.

"Eat all your breakfast, Mister Bert. You won't be getting much food today."

The eggs were plucked right from the chicken coop outside the house and tasted so much better than store-bought ones. I had forgotten how good eggs tasted fresh from the chicken.

I was starting to see the animals around Paz's home—the pigs, ducks, chickens, dogs, cats—in a different way. They were more like family members and companions now, rather than merely noisy intruders who disturbed my spiritual reverie.

I felt more relaxed today, but I was still wondering what I was doing here. Before this, I would have been worried about wasting my time, but that didn't enter my mind. This was actually a perfect setting for me, a classic overachiever—a place to do nothing except be with myself, sweat, and think.

I took a sponge bath after my run and didn't feel any different, since the humidity produced a thick new layer of sweat as soon as I sponged the bath water off.

I thought how easy running would be back home after this tropical initiation.

Paz came upstairs and told me that I would be going with her to a healing service that night at a church in the jungle, about five miles away by car. I lay down under my netting, anticipating the need for rest as the healing service was going to be an all-night affair.

DARK NIGHT IN THE JUNGLE

When we arrived at what was supposed to be the church site, it was around 9:00 PM, and the night had long since lowered its steamy curtain on this place. It was pitch black where Paz parked the car in a small, semicircular clearing at the edge of the dense jungle. It was at this point that I began to question what I had gotten myself into. I seriously contemplated asking her to take me back home so I could wait there until she was through with the service.

This might have been an option had she not treated me like a member of her family and with such gracious hospitality. I just couldn't bring myself to ask her to take me home.

We got out of the car, and Paz reached into the glove compartment, pulled out a flashlight, and stepped into the dense jungle growth alongside the road.

I had to either follow her or stand at the edge of the jungle all night. I moved ahead, hesitating before plunging into the thick undergrowth of the jungle floor.

As the branches and leaves whacked me in the face and tore at my bare arms and legs, I knew immediately that I had a serious wardrobe problem. I was your typical American tourist, since I opted to stay as cool as decency would allow, in shorts, a tank top, and my Birkenstock sandals. Long pants and a long-sleeved shirt would have been a much better jungle uniform.

Besides the small beam from the flashlight in Paz's hand, there wasn't a trace of light or any other indication of human life as I followed close behind her.

I felt like this was not a good place to be as the jungle snapped shut behind us like a Venus Flytrap ensnaring its victims. As the jungle closed around us, it instantly removed any trace of our ever having walked this way. The jungle was alive with sounds that I had never heard before—monkeys chattering, insects singing, howls.

We must have walked at least a quarter of a mile when, through the branches and vines lining our path, I could make out a faint ray of light up ahead. A cheesy cliché flashed in my mind: *Thank you, God! A light at the end of the tunnel!*

I had no idea what I was in for, but seeing this light turned what I figured was healthy suspicion into fear, since now there were sure to be even more people who I thought might be capable of doing some kind of irreversible psychic or spiritual damage to me.

Oh, ye of little faith, I thought to myself.

As we entered the edge of a clearing, the light I saw turned out to be a small, ten-watt bulb hanging from a tree branch. A generator hummed in the background.

As my eyes grew accustomed to the light, I saw twelve to fifteen Filipino spiritualists, all of them very small, less than five feet tall, standing underneath a clear, plastic tarp that measured about twenty feet square and stretched over two rows of ten plain, hardwood benches, each one about ten feet long.

The people were talking softly in Tagalog. They were gathered around a podium that was supported by a five-foot-square platform that lifted the podium about three feet above the jungle floor.

This was the church. There was a six-foot hardwood bench, about three feet high, placed a few feet off to the left of the podium, still under the plastic tarp, that was perpendicular to the rows of benches, as if some kind of healing ceremony or demonstration was conducted there, for all the participants in the congregation to watch.

Something about that bench spoke to me. It said: "It's pretty clear that these people don't often get a chance to work their magic on some guy from Marin County." I was obviously the featured guest here tonight.

Something else told me that I needed to again trust the process, and that I was in good, albeit strange, hands.

The people varied in age from a nineteen-year-old girl to a few men and women in their thirties and forties and up to a tiny little Filipino lady, who looked to be in her seventies or eighties.

This little old one would play a very important role for me that night, in a fashion that I could never have imagined.

The congregation slowly assembled on the benches with the nineteen-year-old standing at the podium, leading the prayers in Tagalog.

Before she started the main body of the prayer, she spoke to the people, and, I assume, told them that I was a special guest, as all heads turned to look in my direction, the eighth row back.

I slowly nodded my head in acknowledgement to them, all the while making sure not to lose eye contact with anyone standing in front of me.

After the introduction, the girl looked up at the top of the clear plastic tarp, as if for guidance, and began to shake visibly for about a minute or so. When she began speaking again, it was in the voice of a much larger, masculine presence, totally different and impossible to fake from the one she had introduced the prayer in.

I felt myself recoil slightly at the power of this new personality. She then moved her hands, which were now continually vibrating, around a compass board that was on the stand in front of her and continued to talk in what sounded to me like tongues.

She preached in this new entity for about two hours with the people chiming in periodically with some kind of Tagalog litany prayer. After she finished the sermon, she shook back into her original form and took her place among the people who were now gathering around a table off to the right of the podium where refreshments appeared.

Socializing took place for about an hour, and then about a third of the people began to leave, fanning out into the jungle in all directions.

It was apparent, to me anyway, that my time had come. The little old lady came toward me from out of the crowd of people that were left, said a few words to me in Tagalog, and motioned for me to follow her.

A SPIRITUAL VACCINATION

The small woman led me over to the bench off to the left of the podium and waved her hand over it, indicating that I should lie down. As I did, the remaining people all gathered around the bench and began to chant softly, not in Tagalog, but in tongues.

That did nothing to quell my fears, even though I felt a gentleness and love in that jungle clearing among these people, the likes of which I had never before felt.

Paz took her place at one side of the bench, and the little lady took her place on the other. Paz held a large Bible in her hands. I looked over at the old one, and someone had handed her the largest syringe I had ever seen.

The needle had to be about eight inches long, and the body of the syringe was at least eighteen inches. Fear swept over me as I began to sweat even more profusely than normal in the steamy jungle air. I had to force myself to return to the feelings of love and compassion I had felt from these people to dispel the fear. That's the only thing that kept me on the bench.

What made it worse was that I couldn't understand a word they were saying leading up to my "ceremony."

The old woman continued to pray over me for what seemed like an hour or so. Her prayers felt to me like she was calling on God to prepare me to receive the healing that I had come for. After that preliminary healing, she then had Paz open the Bible wide. Paz mashed the pages flat, and then the old one placed the needle into the Bible and began to suck energy (this is the only way I can describe it) from the open pages of the Bible until she had the syringe extended all the way back and full of "Bible energy."

Then she placed the needle up against my left arm and began to simulate injecting the withdrawn energy from the Bible into my outstretched arm. I felt a rush of energy flow into my body as she pushed the plunger of the syringe into the barrel.

I felt like I was rising up off the wooden bench as she continued to "inject" the energy into me. Then she did the same thing with my right arm, and I felt myself rise up off the bench once again. During this whole process, the people were chanting and praying softly. Now the chanting comforted me and eased my fears. I sank back onto the bench and relaxed.

After the ceremony, two of the people in the healing group gently helped me off the bench and stood me up. They laughed softly as I wobbled, trying to get my balance. I began to weep as I thought, *Why me, God? Why are they spending so much time and love tending to me?* That was the same feeling I had when I left Babaji in India. *Why me?* I was simply not used to receiving this kind of loving service without feeling unworthy or like I had to return the favor.

The sunlight was just beginning to filter through the dense jungle canopy in a hundred hazy shafts as we walked back to the car for the ride back home. But there was yet another piece to the Philippine puzzle that I needed to learn about.

After arriving back at Paz's home, I slept fitfully for a few hours due to the stifling late-morning heat. Many new thoughts were pouring through my head, so I got up around 10:00 AM and wandered through the village for the remainder of the day. I went to bed again early that night.

The following morning I was up with the chickens after a sleepless night. The good news was the winds had blown all night and forced the mosquitoes to fight a strong crosswind that kept most of them from landing on my net and penetrating my fragile defense system.

I walked down to breakfast. Paz had my eggs, toast, and Tang ready for me. I thanked her deeply for what she had done for me and told her of my intention to travel to Baguio, a village high in the Philippine mountains.

Before I left home in Marin County, I had heard that Baguio was a town where many tourists came for healing, so I decided to go there to see what that place had for me. My time with Paz was complete.

The energy that I received in the jungle clearing that night would continue to build in me until fourteen years later, when I, too, would mount a platform, remember this moment, and do a very different kind of healing.

MOUNTAIN MAGIC

Paz gave me a ride to the bus stop where I caught the 7:30 AM bus to Baguio. I felt lonely and homesick, but with a deeper sense of having gotten some of what I came for after the jungle healing ceremony.

I had no plan for Baguio, or what I would find there. I just knew that some of the most respected and powerful Spiritualist Faith Healers lived and practiced there.

Some unseen force was driving me to see these people who performed surgery and healed disease without any tools except prayer, their hands, and their strong, unadulterated faith in God.

Something had to whack me out of my arrogance and lifelong dependence on left-brain thinking, and point my soul in the direction of a more all-inclusive, holistic approach to healing my life.

I checked in at the Pines Resort in Baguio at 50 percent off their normal room rate, which was eighteen dollars. God bless airline discounts!

After dumping my luggage in the room, I walked around town looking for a sign that would lead me to contact one of the healing tours that might be there.

I thought of one of my childhood buddies, who had married a Filipina woman and was living in his hand-built cabin in the forest somewhere near Baguio. I fantasized about running into him in the hotel lobby bar and having a beer for old times' sake—anything that smacked of familiarity that I could hold onto in lieu of this apparently aimless wandering.

After shuffling around town for two days and watching my mind exhaust all possibility of reasonable expectations, I decided to sit and wait for "it" to come to me.

I didn't have a clue where this journey was taking me. All I knew was that, for the first time in my life, I felt free of somebody else's expectations of me. I think it was about taking life into my own hands for the first time and following what I felt, not thought, was the right thing to do. I began to listen to my heart.

On the morning of the third day, I returned to the hotel lobby and sat down in a large, overstuffed chair where I could see most of the people who came in from the street.

I heard some loud conversation and looked up to see a group of Europeans standing around, looking almost as aimless as me. They were a group of two men and three women, and they were led by an intense, wiry young man with piercing eyes.

When I saw them, something told me to approach them and see if I might tag along wherever they were going.

After watching them for a few minutes, I walked up to the wiry man and introduced myself. He told me his name was Dr. Werner Uhlrich. He was a medical resident from Austria.

When I asked him what they were doing there, he told me, "I heard about the faith healers at the hospital in Austria where I'm in residence. Something about my medical training has left me wondering if there's something more that I can do to help my patients besides just treating their symptoms. So I did some research on what was happening over here and decided to put together a healing tour with some of my sicker patients to see if they might be helped. What brings you here?"

"I'm not really sure. I just know that since my divorce, my life has been turned upside down. It's not as neat and orderly as I thought it was. I got depressed thinking how selfish and lonely I've been."

I told him how I'd gone to India, and how, when I'd returned home, I still felt the need to continue my search for some kind of meaning to my life. I felt like I'd learned something significant in India, but I wasn't sure what it was.

"Well," he told me, "we've arranged a visit to the village of Borangobang in Villasis, Pangasanan, today to visit Josephine Sisson, a healer who lives there. You're welcome to come along if you wish."

I felt my face start to turn red and my heart start to race; tears began to well up in the corners of my eyes. The path was finally being laid out in front of me, and I felt relief and gratitude for trusting my intuition and coming all this way.

This serendipitous meeting with Dr. Uhlrich felt like what was soon to become a common theme in my life, a miraculous meeting where I was much more open to God's leading, much less attached to any particular outcome, and always overwhelmed by the gift of something unexpected, yet significant for my life.

From someone else's perspective, these situations might not seem miraculous, but from my heart's perspective, they confirmed that my life was on the right track. Which track I wasn't always sure, but I had a new ability to trust that where I was being led was exactly where I needed to be.

I looked quickly away from Dr. Uhlrich. I had never felt so much energy coming from my heart before. It felt like my heart was going to jump out of my chest. I gently patted my chest in an unconscious attempt to settle this new surge of energy.

It felt like my heart knew its mission was finally being acknowledged and I had stumbled onto a major piece of its healing.

In following Dr. Ulrich and his medical tourists, I would soon come to know the meaning behind the phrase, "Believe it and you'll see it." My thinking would be rocked and transformed by what I was about to witness in the next few hours.

LEARNING TO TRUST THE HOLY SPIRIT

We all piled into a large Jeepney that Uhlrich had hired. As we started down the main road through town, I felt a heaviness and a feeling of fear. As I would find out later, this trip was a last resort for most of Uhlrich's patients, many of whom had been diagnosed with terminal cancer.

After about five miles traveling out of town on the main paved road, we turned onto the first dirt road before the bridge that led to Carmen, which was on the way from Baguio to Manila.

We drove down the dirt road for about a mile and a half and arrived at Josephine Sisson's home a little before noon that day. Immediately upon stepping out of the car, I heard the Tagalog equivalent of fire-and-brimstone preaching blaring from a little thatched hut alongside the main house.

After we paid the cab driver 900 pesos for our ride, I walked over to the hut to see who was preaching. Inside was the Filipino version of Billy Graham, holding the Bible up in the air, then slamming it on the podium in front of him, and pounding his fist into the center of it to make a point in Tagalog.

As I would find out later, the preacher was emphasizing the need for us to take a hand in our own healing through an unshakeable faith in God and a change in our way of thinking. If not, the disease that these healers would try to cure would continue to manifest itself again and again in our unchanged consciousness upon returning home.

These Filipinos were a curious and wonderful combination of spiritualist, religionist, shaman, medicine person, and mystic all wrapped into one.

According to Jaime Licauco in his book, *The Truth Behind Faith Healing in the Philippines*, the healing powers of the Filipinos is thought to stem from the Philippines itself being a past site of the ancient, mythical, mystical city of Lemuria, the Pacific Ocean counterpart of Atlantis.

I backed slowly away from the hut, so I wouldn't disturb the five or six faithful inside, and then I made my way into Josephine's house, where our little pilgrim party was assembling.

Josephine greeted us in her front room and directed us into a back room that was set aside for healing.

She was about five-foot-four, and she was stocky with a pleasant, round face. Even though I had just come off the experience of seeing Jesus, I was still a bit skeptical about faith healing.

One of Dr. Uhlrich's patients, Helga, lay down on the table. Without any fanfare, Josephine immediately looked up as if in prayer for guidance, shook a bit as she went into a trance, and hovered her hands over Helga's entire body, about six inches above it.

She stopped at Helga's abdomen and, without hesitation, placed both hands onto Helga's stomach. As Josephine continued to pray, her hands appeared to meld into Helga's stomach through an opening that spontaneously appeared. (One "rational" theory, as opposed to the miraculous, unexplainable way of seeing this kind of thing, is that the healer has the ability to match the spiritual "vibration" of the patient's body. This vibrational "compatibility" [my word] allows the two to become one, which then allows the healer's hands to penetrate the body.)

The opening was visible to me as I stood off to her left and behind Josephine, alongside the healing table. There was a small amount of blood as Josephine's fingers penetrated Helga's body up to the knuckles, this being more of an opening than a wound.

Josephine seemed to be feeling for something as she moved her fingers around in the opening. When she removed her hands from the opening, she held something that looked like a bloody garbanzo bean with some stringy material hanging from it.

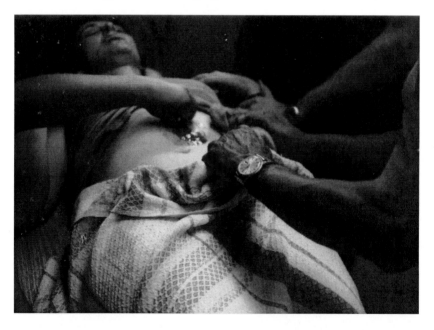

She placed it in an empty tin can that one of her assistants held in his hand. I asked the assistant softly if I could look closer at the diseased body part, and he said, "Yes, but please don't touch it, it's not good."

It looked as if Helga felt no pain. Josephine then passed her hands over the rest of Helga's body and did some work on her legs, again placing her hands on each one of Helga's legs and entering the skin with her fingers, with minimal bleeding. After feeling around just beneath the surface of the skin, she then removed some stringy material that was apparently blocking her circulation and causing varicose veins.

I took a picture of Dr. Ulrich as he watched this. His head was turned half away from the healing scene as if he couldn't, or didn't want to, believe what he was seeing.

Josephine then motioned for Helga to get up slowly off the table and go sit in another, outer room.

Josephine then placed one of the other patients, an old man, on the table and scanned his body. His problem was severe cataracts and, as she scanned the area around his eyes, she started massaging his eyes and then removed one of them from the socket.

I couldn't believe what I was seeing, yet it was so effortless and without fanfare that what I was witnessing had to be happening. I saw the eyeball in her hands with a bunch of stringy material that I can only imagine was nerve endings hanging from the eyeball. She then appeared to wash the eyeball in some solution and replaced it in the old man's socket. She did the same to his other eyeball as well.

When the old man got up off the table, his vision had been restored, which is when the impact of what I had been witnessing overcame me. I began to cry, feeling an overwhelming sense of compassion for these people and gratitude for being allowed to witness what I can only describe as spontaneous, miraculous healing.

I have no idea how or why these healings occurred; suffice it to say that I saw something in this village, twelve thousand miles from home, that changed the way that I reasoned about the world and how I perceived reality.

I now had answers to questions that I didn't even know I had or was able to articulate. I knew something about the healing process now that would help me trust that I had something of my own to offer a world in need.

After about an hour and a half, all the Austrians had taken their turn on Josephine's healing table. I walked out to the little shack where the church service had been held. I asked one of Josephine's other assistants to hail us a couple of cabs for the ride back to Baguio.

I stood in the motley crew of healees and the doctor, and we waited in the dirt by the side of the road for one of the local cabs to show. We were contemplative and quiet. I figured that there would be some joy, some celebration, or something that these people, who had traveled halfway around the world, would express. But there was not so much as a peep out of them.

We climbed into the cab, and I headed for the back seat next to the doctor while the old man and Helga sat in the front. We got about three blocks out of the small town, and I could hear Helga's occasional soft, muffled sobs. I leaned forward from my position in the back seat and saw the old man sitting in the front seat, looking out the window, and smiling quietly as if he were seeing the jungle rushing by for the first time.

I felt a mixture of joy, because the old man got what he came for, and sadness, because Helga knew that her healing would probably only be temporary.

When we arrived back at the Pines Resort, I said my goodbyes to Uhlrich and the other Austrians with a promise to develop the pictures I had taken of their healing sessions and send them off once I arrived back in the States.

Before checking out of my room, I went to the front desk to pick up some laundry that I had left before our journey to Borangobang. When the bellboy brought the cleaning back to me and I opened the package, the shirts I had left with the people at the front desk had been laundered, pressed, and folded with such loving care that I began to shake with sobs right there in the lobby.

Something about seeing that my crummy, light blue chambray shirt and filthy shorts had been laundered with such love by these people released the flood of tears that represented the gratitude and love that I felt for having been blessed with my life, as well as the opportunity to travel to this place, to have these experiences, and to tend to my soul's purpose in this way.

My tears dripped from my face and began to spread into gentle, flowing stains on the neatly pressed shirts. I felt like I was being baptized with the healing waters of my newly awakened soul.

It was now clear to me that this journey to Josephine's with the Austrians was one of the reasons I came to the Philippines.

Something would continue to shift in how I saw the world and walked in it after this. The need that I used to have for hard data was being replaced with a new trust in a loving God that helped to alleviate my need to have it all together, look good at all costs, and not screw up. Alas, I would continue to screw up, but now I was able to take responsibility for it and not blame anyone else.

I was able to now follow a flight plan that called for more "seat-of-the-pants flying" than ever before.

The flight back to the U.S. from Manila was routine, but there were no open rows of seats for me to get some sleep in. I had lots of time to reflect on the power of my trip and its effect on me.

I learned that "believing is seeing." I saw things during my time with the Filipino healers that my mind didn't understand, but my heart knew was possible and existed outside the constraints of a belief system that was slowly unraveling.

These were my CEUs (continuing education units) in relying less on logic and trusting my heart, which was slowly expanding to include someone besides myself. God would enhance and qualify that deepening, healing part of me even more in a few short years.

CHAPTER 12

SAVING THE WORLD, ONE MAN'S HEART AT A TIME

When I returned home from the Philippines, I was unable to return to "life as usual." I still loved flying and the people I had spent the last fifteen years of my life with, but I had seen things and felt the power of transformation that stirred my need to give back in some way. But how?

I resumed my flying career, but I was restless; flying was no longer an all-consuming passion for me, as it had been before.

I don't remember where or how I learned about the Transpersonal Counseling Master's degree program that John F. Kennedy University in Orinda, California, offered, but I remember that when I read the curriculum, I knew it was just what I wanted. Babaji and the people of India had begun opening my heart, and the Philippines opened it further, and upon my return, I now had room for something besides my own self-absorbed pain.

The rest of the three years in the program went by quickly. I graduated from JFK University in 1984 with a Master's degree in Counseling Psychology. I couldn't have forecasted that I would be able to attend 90 percent of my classes and still fly for my airline. That was made possible by my bidding flights as a reserve pilot. That meant I was on call much of the time. I carried a beeper everywhere I went, had my bags packed, and kept my uniform in the trunk of my car.

Shortly after graduating from JFK, I met a woman, Lani, who would become my fourth wife. She was an art therapist, and we met through mutual friends. We started dating and soon moved into a beautiful home together on a small lake in the hills above Skyline Boulevard, overlooking the Bay Area.

We both knew that I would be leaving soon to live in Miami to do some postgraduate studies in the Psychology of Mind. I did not want to make this move alone, such was the extent of my need to have a woman in my life as some kind of emotional lifeline.

So Lani moved with me to Miami. We were married there a few months after I settled into the postgraduate work. Lani would eventually join me in the Psychology of Mind course work, too.

She turned out to be my fourth and final "learning experience" marriage before the truly miraculous transformation I would experience en route to the meeting of my present wife, but for now, we'll stay with the story of my ongoing journey toward transformation.

Twelve years had passed since I'd been in the Philippines. I had a Master's Degree in Counseling Psychology, I had upgraded to captain at TWA after a twenty-three-year "apprenticeship," and Lani and I were living in Miami.

But there were still gaps in my soul's development. I was still searching for something, but I wasn't sure what. I'd always been a late bloomer, but this was stretching the point.

From Miami, Lani and I moved to St. Louis, Missouri, TWA's hub at the time. I had been awarded a captain position on the DC9 and MD80 aircraft that necessitated the move.

Lani and I were a complete mismatch. I knew from the beginning that I had made a mistake in marrying her. My emotional neediness overshadowed any semblance of wisdom in picking a wife.

Shortly after we moved to St. Louis, we both realized that our relationship was dead, and that it was killing us as well. We mutually agreed to a separation. Lani moved back to her family on the East Coast, and I stayed in St. Louis.

We divorced in 1995. I didn't consider myself much further along the road to enlightenment than when I "officially" kicked off my spiritual journey to India after my third divorce in 1980. This felt more like the Road to Perdition than a path to enlightenment.

One could say that lack of follow-through after my initial epiphany had left me flapping in the cold winds of fate. Or, one could say that it was not yet my time. I had either backslid badly from my earlier awakening, or I was in the throes of a lengthy spiritual germination period. I prefer to think that the latter was true.

In late August 1992, I arrived at a place called Wellspring, thirty-five minutes from downtown Milwaukee in the Milwaukee River Valley. As strange as it may sound to men less in need of male love and acceptance, I was there to take yet another step in my attempt to become a loved, loving, significant man.

I was drawn to this remote site in northern Wisconsin by a magazine ad inviting men to attend a "powerful adult male rite-of-passage training." I was fifty-three years old, successful in a flying and a counseling career, and yet, I was still seeking something that would assuage the gnawing feeling that something was not right with my soul.

This training would hopefully point me in the direction of fulfilling my life's purpose and finding my place as a man in a culture that I feel has virtually obliterated a healthy, nurturing identity for most men.

I was at this place in the woods because something in the literature describing this weekend initiation spoke to my need as a man to be accepted and loved by other healthy men—men who had done their work in plumbing the depths of their own souls for meaning.

I was seeking something that I had never received from the men in my life—my father, most of my teachers in school, the men whom I flew with. Only Uncle Pete and Lt. McGill had ever awakened and nurtured this dormant need in me.

I needed to feel connected to other men who would help me heal the disconnectedness I felt from my own father. This weekend was about men taking a look at their shadows in the company of a staff of thirty or more other men who had done this training before, and who had now returned to offer the gift of themselves to initiates like me.

The shadow is that dark part of our psychological makeup that we've buried deep in our psyche. If left unattended, it can, and will, put a negative spin on just about everything we do. The term "shadow" was coined by C. J. Jung, the brilliant Austrian psychoanalyst after whom Jungian psychology was named.

Throughout the three years I was in graduate school, I had never heard of the concept of the shadow. This work was new to me, but I could tell right away that I needed it.

This weekend would show me how this shadow affected everything I had ever done and would do in my life—from the way I related to women, to the misuse of my male power, to my need for recognition, to my arrogance, up through and beyond my need to look better than others because of my insecurities.

These things weren't promised in the weekend literature, but this is what I recognized in myself after I completed the training and started the subsequent process of integrating what I had learned about myself during the weekend.

The temperature in this part of Wisconsin wasn't nearly as hot as that Himalayan village I'd studied in twelve years earlier. But something told me that the ambient temperature was hardly an indication of the transformative heat that would cook my emotional and spiritual beans at this remote place.

Even though I had done lots of soul-searching between my time in India and the Philippines, and had attended many personal growth and spiritual conferences and seminars, both as a participant and a leader, and had prayed in the best ways I knew how in Lakota sweat lodges, something was still missing. I was only now, at midlife, beginning to get that the journey was much more important than any destination. The healing that I had received in the Philippine jungle would soon reveal its use as I plunged headlong into the world of men's healing.

At fifty-three years old, and with the fourth failed marriage gnawing at my self-esteem, I was loaded with personal shame.

I needed to know how to be a healthy, loving, nurturing man. Not the wimpy SNAG (sensitive, new age guy) kind that were overcompensating for the sixties feminist movement, but an authentic, truthful, strong man who was powerful in a gentle, wise way, befitting my rapidly approaching elder status.

I had been given the gift of manhood, but it was wrapped so tightly that I wasn't able to unravel it.

I knew what the next step was. I felt like I was divinely guided to this place, but I was petrified of digging into that dark part of me. That would mean exposing what I had kept so well hidden from not only myself, but also from the women who saw my heart's potential and had hung with me to the bitter end.

This kind of social disease had kept me from being fully functional in a world that encouraged and supported none of this kind of self-exploration and congruency.

AM I GOOD ENOUGH?

My Uncle Pete had started the process. Lieutenant McGill had taken it to another level. Even after my experience at the feet of Babaji, however, I still needed to be unconditionally accepted as an equal into a community of men—men who would accept me just as I was, men with whom I could share the parts of me that were scared, that weren't sure of myself, that bumbled my way through relationships. I needed those parts of me to be seen without them being used against me. I needed to be able to trust men who could love me in a healthy way that no man ever had. As a man in our culture, these things are not easy to find.

As it turned out, this training would erase much of the old feelings of my not being good enough, a feeling that colored everything I had done in my life up to now—from well before my reluctance to apply to navy flight training, through my failed relationships, and into the fear that I felt as I would ready myself for my airline captain training in 1989.

I still feel twinges of that same fear when I set out to do something that triggers that feeling of not being good enough. That voice inside of me says, "You aren't smart enough to do that," or, "You can't do that alone; you need someone to teach you how to do it," or, "You don't have what it takes."

My heroes, the men I flew with in the navy and the airlines, the men whom I wanted to emulate—the Naval Academy-graduate fighter pilots, whom I saw as better and brighter than me—all had their unique brand of Achilles heel that they, too, hid well.

We had all mastered the art of self-deception by covering up our feelings of fear and inadequacy. We pretend to look like we have it all together. We're cool, baby. We swagger and joke and deflect any inquiry as to how we're really feeling.

And that bottling up of our true feelings continues to kill most of us long before our missions are complete because our hearts attack us for not allowing them to express themselves.

THE HUMAN HEART

The heart is the primary life-giving organ in the body; it's also the closest thing to the seat of our emotions and the vehicle for our soul's expression. A man who bottles up his real feelings only accelerates the rate at which his heart might attack him—in too many cases, long before his true, God-given mission in life is complete.

This training would include a look at what my life's mission was, what the full expression of my passion as a man in the world might look like if I had the insight, courage, and support to pursue it. It would also mean that I would have to peel back the mask that I had hidden behind for my whole life, and reveal those parts of me that I considered unlovable and ugly and that I had repressed for so long.

The women I'd coupled with over the years knew what I'd tried to keep hidden, the wounded parts, the ugly parts. But they also saw something that allowed them to hang in with me long after they should have abandoned me as an emotional lost cause. I hurt them because I wouldn't, or couldn't, be an integral part of their lives.

I needed to be initiated as a man into a brotherhood that went beyond the normal competitive, sports-oriented, ass-kickin', girl-cha-sin', beer-drinkin' fraternity that had been my experience. I never felt like I belonged to any of this, and yet I kept trying to conform to some unwritten, Western male code of conduct.

My initiation had to go beyond the current vestigial cobwebs of male initiation that continue to hang impotently from the rafters of modern-day religion such as confirmation, bar mitzvah, fraternity rushing, and such.

I had bottled up my anger at my own impotence because I was afraid if I let it out, I would rage out of control and kill someone. The cruel joke was that I continued to perpetuate the rage by turning my self-resentment inward through a lack of acknowledgement and expression of that poison. Then, through self-judgment honed to perfection over the years, the self-hate festered, and the cycle continued.

My mantra became: "We are masters of negative self-judgment, since we're our own best (worst) critics."

RELEASING THE FLOODGATES OF RAGE, ANGER, AND UNWORTHINESS

The New Warrior training was designed by men who had felt the same need to be initiated as I did. The majority of men in our culture are devoid of any means to express this need.

All of the weekend exercises were carefully crafted to flesh out long-held feelings of rage, anger, shame, sadness, and fear.

The process then facilitated shining the light of awareness on these feelings and transmuting the energy trapped in negativity into joy, creativity, and nurturance of self and others.

One of the exercises that would later become my favorite to facilitate as a weekend leader myself was designed to prod a man's "guts" to get him to release deeply held feelings.

This was necessary in order to bring to the surface all the psychological stuff that keeps us stuck, that keeps us repeating the same old destructive patterns time and time again.

I was so ready to rid myself of the pain and anger I had carried for so long that when the drum sounded for the first man to step onto the carpet to do his emotional "guts" work, I automatically leapt into the center of the room.

As I took my place on the carpet—that symbolic, sacred, grubby place in the center of the floor where men did their emotional work on these weekends—the leader probed gently, firmly, and expertly for ways into my pain. I had a spontaneous flashback to a time, at age nine, when my pop and I were playing catch with a baseball and mitts in the backyard of our home on Flood Street in San Francisco.

The day was typically cold and windy. I would try to please Pop by throwing the ball straight to him, so he wouldn't have to chase it.

When I did make an inevitable bad throw, he would retrieve the ball, place it in his mitt, and walk back into the house saying, "If you can't throw the Goddamn ball good enough so I don't have to chase it, then I'm not going to play with you anymore."

Instantly, I remembered the pain of rejection that I felt from the man whom I wanted so much to be my hero.

As the staff man whom I picked to play my "bad dad" taunted me by walking away, pounding an imaginary ball into an imaginary mitt, I charged after him in a rage. It took six other staff men to hold me back.

I didn't know it at the time, but a path was being augered open in my heart to allow the poisonous bile of self-hate, resentment, and shame to flow out.

I would carry the burden of being "not good enough" for many years to come because of my father's insistence that I play perfect catch.

In my mind as a little boy, I wasn't good enough to play with him. I wasn't smart enough; I didn't learn quickly enough; I wasn't fast enough. I know now that those admonitions weren't true. But as a nine-year-old boy, my survival was totally dependent on my father's approval.

His words of criticism were all I knew about myself at that age. His words pierced my heart, seared themselves into my mind, and became my reality for much of my adult life.

I didn't know enough at nine to think that my father's father had most likely treated him the same way, and that he was merely passing on the family legacy to me.

In this moment, freeze-framed in my mind like images in time-lapse photography, I saw myself as an actor playing a leading role in my own movie. I saw how I spoke the lines and acted the part that I had so methodically learned.

After the rage subsided and the tears ceased flowing, men whom I had learned to trust with my life during that short weekend held me in their arms, stroked my head, and told me things that I had always longed to hear from my pop and never did... and never would.

I felt the healing from these men's gentle words penetrate deep into my heart, their effect cauterizing my emotional wounds. They pierced the venomous abscess of fear and rage. The emotional pus drained onto that grubby, old carpet.

That poison was replaced by a joy, a lightness of being, and a feeling of freedom that I could now dance and play, anytime, anywhere, and in front of anyone; I would never again be afraid of being judged for who I am.

From that time forward, I would know that soaring like the joyful eagle that I had become was my birthright. I would leave the fear, the worry, and the frustration to the earthbound, clipped-winged chickens of the world.

The angels I had known before this weekend were inanimate carved statues mounted high on pedestals or majestically depicted in elaborate paintings in the churches of my youth.

Those men in the weekend training were the first angels that I had met who wore Levis and T-shirts, swore, drank beer, and openly loved me. Yet they carried similar wounds as mine.

This experience was so sacredly profound, yet smacked of enough real-world profanity that I knew I had found my heart's path.

SOFT EYES IN THE AIRPORT JUNGLE

During the short time between attending the New Warrior training and returning to my flying career, I had an experience that brought home the power of transformation that I had gone through.

My TWA flight crew—myself, the copilot, and three flight attendants—had just gotten out of the hotel van after our twenty-four hour layover at the downtown Philadelphia Sheraton hotel. We had worked a flight from San Francisco to Philadelphia, and we were now arriving at the Philadelphia Airport to fly nonstop back home to San Francisco.

When the van dropped us off in front of the terminal, I picked up my bags from the curb, walked over to the large glass doors leading into the terminal, and nudged one of the doors open with my foot.

My copilot and I carried our layover luggage and a large crew kit, called a "brain bag." This bag contained our flight manuals, flashlights, navigation manuals, and everything else essential to the flight.

This was in the days before wheeled luggage became popular, so I was lugging my two bags, one in each hand, like a long-armed, uniformed gorilla. I headed for the escalator that would take us to the upper terminal.

That morning, I had meditated in my hotel room before going flying, and I felt unusually "grounded" (in a good way for a pilot!) and centered.

I was unusually aware of and in touch with my surroundings and without any kind of noticeable expectations.

As I stepped onto the escalator, I happened to notice a large woman a few steps ahead of me who was carrying a baby and fumbling with the baby's stroller. As the escalator steps uncoiled from their invisible metal nest, a strap on the stroller got caught in the steps.

As the mother attempted to free the stroller from the steps, she tripped and started to fall backwards. I saw her falling toward me in slow motion. In an instant, I had thrown my bags over the escalator railing, stopped the woman's fall, and grabbed the baby in my arms.

I continued to hold the woman up until we got to the top of the escalator, and then handed the baby back to her without any particular fanfare. Then I walked back down the stairs that paralleled the escalator and retrieved my bags. My brain bag had burst open and spilled its contents all over the bottom steps: airport approach charts, flight computers, pens, pencils, and a protein bar, amongst other things.

As my crew continued our walk through the terminal and to the gate where our aircraft awaited us, my fellow crewmembers, who had witnessed this whole incident because they were either behind me on the escalator or walking up the stairs that paralleled the escalator, commented on how quickly I acted. They asked me how I knew what to do.

I had no clue as to how I reacted the way I did. All I know is that because of my relaxed state of awareness and the lack of extraneous thoughts, quite possibly due to my prior meditation, my eyes were naturally "soft," my peripheral vision was all-encompassing, and I was in what a former Himalayan teacher called a state of "thoughtless awareness."

I was in the zone. Athletes that attain altered states of consciousness and achieve extraordinary feats have explained that there are ways of perceiving ourselves, each other, and our world that can enable us to extend our boundaries. We can go beyond our limits and experience a rewarding oneness both within and without.

In some inexplicable way, I had succeeded in channeling the adrenaline-based fight-or-flight response that we inherited from primitive man in order to survive in the wilds of nature, and I used it in a modern-day response of service through awareness.

It wouldn't be long before I recognized that my flying days were over and I would heed the call to initiation; the call to something that would use more of my newly awakened gifts was imminent.

CHAPTER 13

GIVING BACK

One of my all-time best "everyday miracles" was about to happen. I completed the men's initiation training in August of 1992. Before leaving for the weekend training, I had known about a buyout, accompanied by a discounted retirement package, that was being offered to the more senior pilots at my airline.

Even though I loved my flying career and the men and women I'd spent most of my life with, I had become increasingly bored with the kind of flying I was doing. It felt like I was just flying back and forth across the country, looking out the window, wondering if this was still my calling.

When I returned to St. Louis from Milwaukee, I knew I needed to immerse myself in this new environment with the kind of men I'd been on retreat with and the deep emotional healing that I had experienced on the weekend.

The timing couldn't have been any better had I hired God as my event planner! On October 31, 1992, I scooped up my retirement monies and with nary a glance in the rearview mirror of my flying life, I walked away from the best career any man who loved flying could have had.

Something about the work I'd experienced with the New Warrior group offered me enough of a spiritual safety net to leave flying. It also strengthened my resolve to serve, to give back to a world that I had taken too much from. This work also bolstered my knowing that I would be taken care of without the illusive security of my flying career.

SERVICE

I had found something in this men's healing work that addressed my need to give something back, so after I left my flying career, I decided to apprentice as a staff man in this work, with the intention to pursue leadership within the organization.

When I returned to St. Louis, I started to talk to people about what I had experienced and my need for the kind of emotional healing I had received in the New Warrior training. I talked to men in St. Louis bookstores, in libraries, in churches. I talked to whomever would listen.

As a result, word spread. One or two men traveled to other cities and trickled through the New Warrior training. They returned with the same fire in their bellies that I had. We began to meet and share our experiences, our visions for our lives and this work in St. Louis.

I continued to staff trainings in cities around the world. I used my free airline passes to travel to trainings throughout the U.S. and Europe. It was one year later that I was chosen to act first as a coleader and then, after three years, as a fully certified leader. Before I was able to lead a training, I had to learn the comprehensive craft of providing a safe enough "container" (the intentional space that the staff creates, so men who come to the weekend as initiates feel safe enough to go deep into their unexplored emotions and feelings).

This work was essential for fanning the embers of spirituality that burn deep within the caverns of all men's souls. Over the course of the first few years that I staffed, working at least four to five trainings a year, I discovered something that I believe to this day.

After seeing so many men's hearts open while working with them and receiving the gifts of their new enthusiasm for life, their openness, and the joy that they now had, I believe that men are at least as capable as women, and in some cases moreso, of expressing their love for one another. The heart opening is the key.

Even though the New Warrior training wasn't meant to be religious, something about the work of stripping away the layers of veneer around a man's heart inevitably leads him to discover his own version of spirituality.

I wasn't aware at the time of how God would show up later in my life. I only knew that something or someone bigger, someone much larger and more in charge, was pulling the strings on my life. It was not unlike the second step in the Alcoholics Anonymous twelve-step program: "We came to believe that a power greater than ourselves could restore us to sanity."

It was obvious in the weekend training that if we set the intention for miracles to happen, prepared the sacred "container of safety" well enough, got our own egos and judgments out of the way, and trusted the process, that healing would inevitably occur.

The healing of men's hearts spoke to me like flying spoke to my need for speed. Except now, in order to complete my healing, I'd have to throttle back and proceed at a much slower, more deliberate, and heart-felt pace.

NEW COURAGE

I had lived too much of my life in fear. It was time to trust the gift of healing that I had been given and step into the unknown. Besides, I was suddenly bored by my flying job that had defined me for twenty-six years; I had to stay true to the promise I had made to myself when I started flying: "If it ever ceases to be fun, I will do something else."

Yet flying as an airline pilot for a quarter-century had served me well. Toward the end of my career, I had ridden the magic carpet of free airline travel, chasing answers to the unknown questions in my heart. That same magic carpet would also serve the men for whom I would act as leader in some fifty-plus subsequent worldwide initiation trainings.

Very often, a vision of a man's ideal world emerged from the weekend training. My vision as a leader was to make a safe place for men, where they could be totally heard without judgment and without the pressure of time. This vision emerged out of my need to be heard as a kid; I was never acknowledged for my intelligence or my input.

I adopted this phrase for myself and for other men: "Don't just do something, sit there!" Men would be able to just hang with other men and laugh, talk, eat, play, and love together with a feeling of being safe to do so, without competing, without trying to outdo one another.

Work would be secondary to play, there would be no time pressure to do anything, no one would control what we did, and we would lie around together a couple of times a day, dreaming our dreams and seeing how we could bring those dreams to reality.

Men who never would have crossed the threshold of a therapist's office would be healed; the results from the weekend trainings in men's lives would render years of therapy unnecessary.

One of the men who attended the training had carried a twenty-five-year burden of guilt for having killed four of his own men under orders from a higher-ranking officer in Vietnam. To say that this man felt relief after our training is a gross understatement. He went on to become a leader in this work.

Men learned to laugh at their screwups rather than attempt to cover them up for fear that they would be ridiculed. I spilled a Coke in my lap in an airport restaurant en route home from a weekend training. To my surprise, I laughed at my clumsiness instead of reacting with anger at my "stupidity," which is how I would have reacted before.

This work made leaving my twenty-six-year flying career a gift instead of generating the fear it might have, had I not seen clearly what I was meant to do. I now had a worldwide community of men that I was an instant and intimate part of.

A man once shared that "I've lost all fear, and that scares the shit out of me…!"

NATURE AS TEACHER

The gifts of my newly opened heart were many. I learned to look for messages in nature. On one of my now more frequent walks in nature, I was in Rockwood forest preserve, about twenty miles southwest of St. Louis. I was looking a long way down a trail that was totally covered with leaves, so much so that I couldn't make out where the trail was leading me.

But the leaf-strewn trail was made up of so many beautiful colors that all of a sudden I realized it wasn't important to know where the trail led, since the beauty of the leaves made the journey itself so beautiful. It was reassuring to know that my path in life was composed of so much beauty.

When I walked in the newly fallen snow of that same forest in another season, I saw animal tracks that were crisp, clean, natural, and well-balanced, and they often appeared to wander aimlessly and yet arrived where they needed to.

How many of us leave tracks that are so clearly read? My tracks have been mostly blurred, clumsy, wandering, confused.

There is a healing power that emerges in a man's heart when he recognizes and acknowledges the beauty and uniqueness of other men and how much more can be accomplished by cooperating and working together. Thankfully, this often translates into a man being more cooperative and available to the women in his life, his kids, and all other living beings.

IN NO RUSH TO BE LIKE MY POP

My pop died at age seventy-five, after vegetating in a coma for forty days. He suffered a broken brain stem in a fall from the roof of our family home in San Francisco.

He was descending on a ladder, propped up from the front porch to the roof of our home, when he fell fifteen feet onto the cold, hard, concrete sidewalk. He had been checking on a roofing job that the workers had just finished.

The lady across the street saw him lying on the sidewalk and called 911. When the emergency medical technicians arrived, they hung a tag on his big toe, estimating his age at fifty-five, twenty years less than his actual age.

Pop had an enormous, untamed, and unchanneled energy. Something inside of me knows that he fell because he was rushing to finish his inspection. This rushing, this unfocused, frenetic energy and need to accomplish something, God knows what, has been passed on to me. I must be constantly aware, else I suffer a similar fate.

That awareness would surface at various times, one of which was when I was flying. Often, the airport tower traffic controller would issue a "cleared for immediate takeoff" clearance as we were taxiing out, approaching the takeoff runway.

Whenever that happened, my first inclination would be to tell the copilot, "Yeah, tell him we can do it. Let's go."

But in that same instant, something deep inside of me would remember what killed Pop: his need to rush and get things done. And I would shake my head and tell my copilot, "Tell him we'll wait."

Many times in those fifty-plus trainings that I staffed and led, I would feel my pop's presence in the room, as if he finally was approving of me.

After I experienced what it was like to express the feelings that I had bottled up for fifty-three years and to feel the love that now flowed freely from my heart, I knew that men's healing was my life's work. I also knew that I had uncovered some of the gifts inside of me that I could now offer other men.

I began to piece together the meaning of my apparently random global wanderings, and how they each contributed to this work I had discovered; the mentorship of my Uncle Pete and Lt. McGill, the affirmation by Babaji in India, and the biblical spiritual healing in the Filipino jungle had led me to this time and place.

CHAPTER 14
IT'S A GOD THING

After six years of leadership and total social and spiritual immersion in the most important community of my life, I left the New Warrior community in 1998. I left this group of men whom I loved and trusted, and who loved, trusted, and supported me.

When someone asks me why I left, I usually answer, "Because it was time." I got what I came for. I achieved what I wanted to achieve: leadership in an organization that provided me with growth, love, challenge, honesty, and support like I had never known before.

The rapid advancement I achieved affirmed what I was never quite sure of in my life: that I excelled as a leader who brought purpose and meaning to my life and to the lives of thousands of other men. I was on my way to becoming extraordinary.

But the real answer to why I left this group of men was that I didn't know how to bring the men under my leadership to God within the structure of the organization as it existed.

It wasn't that the work didn't open men's eyes and hearts to a new awareness of their spiritual nature. It surely did that. But, at age fifty-eight at the time, I was feeling the stirrings of that experience in the Filipino jungle seventeen years earlier, that injection of biblical energy that would eventually make itself known as a call to bring men to God.

The problem was, I was unable to do that yet, since I hadn't found God in my own life.

HEADIN' WEST

I left St. Louis in 1996. I loved St. Louis and the men and women who had become my surrogate family, but I tired of the Midwest and needed to head west. I was, however, still passionate about the men's work that had changed my life.

I stopped for a few years in Taos, New Mexico, where, still as a certified New Warrior leader, I gathered men who had straggled away from their training as New Warriors into integration groups. These were men living in New Mexico who had been initiated as New Warrior brothers, but who had not made contact with other initiated men in order to be part of the integration phase of the New Warrior work.

Those weekly or biweekly integration meetings were the essential continuation of the powerful weekend initiation experience that the men had participated in.

Without this follow-up, the weekend training would be just another experience instead of a life-changing, life-sustaining, ongoing community of like-minded men and their partners.

Northern New Mexico was also a great place to ride the stable of motorcycles I had irresponsibly but enjoyably spent too much of my retirement money on.

LIFESTYLES OF THE PILOTS WHO FLY THE RICH AND FAMOUS

My four years in Taos went quickly, and in 2000, it was clear that I couldn't continue to squander the meager retirement money I had taken away from my twenty-six years at TWA.

I needed to go back to work. The only thing I could do to make a decent, immediate income was to fly airplanes.

Since I had been given travel privileges on TWA after my retirement, I used to commute frequently to St. Louis from Albuquerque to see friends and to reconnect with the New Warrior community there.

On one flight, I was talking to the captain, an old flying buddy of mine. He told me that as soon as he retired from TWA on his sixtieth birthday, the then-mandatory retirement age for airline pilots, he would then begin working at Executive Jet.

Executive Jet is now called Netjets. It was, and still is, the world's most recognized and largest fractional jet ownership company. (Think time-share in corporate jets.)

The private jet travel industry was starting to grow rapidly from the late 1990s up through the mid-2000s, and they needed qualified pilots to keep up with the demand.

It was also becoming clear at that time that my mother was going to be unable to stay in her home and care for herself much longer. Commuting to any of Executive Jet's existing pilot bases from Taos would be next to impossible without the long drive alongside the Rio Grande River to Albuquerque.

A plan was forming. I would move into my mother's home in San Francisco to care for her. If I got hired at Executive Jet, I would commute from San Francisco to whatever pilot base I got hired into. At the time, Executive Jet had only a few pilot bases.

The pilot base that I was hired into was Las Vegas. In those pre-9/11 days, pilots were able to easily "jump-seat," or hitch a ride in one of the empty cockpit seats on most any airline.

I often jump-seated on what was then National Airlines from San Francisco to Las Vegas. Some of my Executive Jet buddies, ex-TWA pilots who had been hired at Exec Jet, had rented a crash pad in Las Vegas. I contacted them and paid my rent, and my living arrangements while waiting for flight assignments were handled.

A short time later, Executive Jet opened up more pilot bases, and one of them was in San Francisco.

As I settled into my new career flying the rich and famous, something would soon take place that would change my life forever and bring me face to face with why I had been racing through life.

Beginning with the hot rods of my youth, continuing on through my life as an airline pilot, through my trek in the mountains of the Himalayas, then sitting at the foot of the guru, and in the jungles of the Philippines, and lying in the beds of so many women while I continued looking for love in all the wrong places, my seeking days would soon come to a screeching halt.

What would be my *raison d'etre*—my reason for existence—if I no longer had the journey to fulfill me? What if I had arrived at the destination?

IT WAS A GOD THING

It was August of 2004. I had been working with a writing coach who had become a friend of mine. After one of our sessions, he said to me, "Bert, there's a man coming to town whom I think you should meet."

Doug knew I had been a spiritual seeker for many years, so he felt comfortable recommending that I meet this man. I agreed, and when Rob came to town, I met with him for an hour or so. We talked about my life and my relationship with God. At the end of the meeting, he asked if he could pray for me. I flippantly said, "Sure Rob, I can always use the help."

So he laid his hands on me and began to pray. When he called on the name of Jesus Christ to "heal your son, Bert," I started to cry. I cried for maybe five minutes or so, and, after I was through, we ended the meeting.

When I left the home where Rob had prayed over me, I knew something had changed. I knew that all the seeking, all the guru-chasing, all the doubting about my spiritual heritage was over. I had found my guru, and it was the God of my Christian youth! I had flown the great circle route, arriving back at the exact point where I had started.

I had come from the Catholicism of my youth, through my relationship with Babaji in the Himalayan mountains, to the Filipino jungle spiritualists and faith healers and beyond, and back to the improbable personal relationship with Jesus Christ.

Prior to this, He had been hidden behind the robes, miters, and habits, the pomp and circumstance, and the irrelevance of too many of Catholicism's well-meaning priests and nuns.

Don't get me wrong. I inherited much of the spirit of these well-intentioned, dedicated clergy, but for much of the time, they stood between me and the Jesus that I was about to spend the rest of my life getting to know.

There is not enough space in this entire book to convey the profound significance that Jesus has had on my life. Suffice it to say that the game changed significantly for me after meeting The God-Man.

But there was another piece of the relationship puzzle that needed to be put in place before I could graduate from my thirty-year relationship "boot camp."

I would only now begin to understand the reasons for the everyday miracles acting as signposts along my way.

IN SERVICE TO WOMEN

I was sixty-six years old when I met Gail. I couldn't afford to fritter away any more of my life, bouncing from one unconscious relationship to another. I saw into that dark tunnel, and I knew that if I kept this pattern going, at the other end was a lonely, bitter old man.

Gail and I met when we both attended a writer's workshop in the hills of San Anselmo, Marin County. I wasn't looking for a relationship at the time. I had entered into a time of isolation, relative silence, and prayer, so that I would be able to eventually do the next right relationship thing.

I was instantly drawn to Gail's intelligence, her joy for life, her British accent, and her red-haired beauty. So much of what I saw in her was what I had missed in my past relationships. Could it be that I was getting closer to my ideal woman?

After my recent experience with Jesus, I knew that I was ready for a God-based relationship. I was hungry to put my new awareness to the test.

But, as is so often the case, this new relationship wouldn't be anything like I thought it would be. It would be more about giving up any preconceived notion of how I thought love was supposed to play out. Instead, what I found was a place inside of my heart that had been gradually wrenched open over the many years of my search. I found that I had minimal expectations of this woman and a maximum need to serve her after I discovered who she was. It would turn out that she had something like a bipolar mental problem.

What was replacing the expectations of what I could get from her was a place inside of me that treasured serving this woman as she slowly began to dissolve emotionally over the next year.

Gail and I dated for about a year and a half, until it became clear that I needed to leave the relationship.

But during that time, I learned more about being of true service to a woman than ever before. I also learned that God had done some serious work in my heart, and that this relationship was one of the ways this new ability to love was being put to the test.

I saw Gail through hospitalizations and rehab for her mental problems. I supported her with money that I was making at my new Netjets job when she was unable to work. I made her a priority in my life simply because she was there, I was there, and it was clear that's what she needed. It was simply about my ability to be present with her at that point in the confluence of our lives.

I knew during the time I was with her that I would never get most of that money back, but that didn't matter. For the first time in my life, I gave with no expectation of getting anything in return.

This was a first for me. And it would turn out to be a futile, but rewarding effort on my part. It was during this time that I saw how this woman had been placed in my life to teach me some final lessons of service before I was ready for the woman who would soon become my wife.

My relationship with Gail ended when we both realized we had done the best we could for and with each other, and that we needed to go our separate ways. I felt at that point that she was at least capable of standing on her own two feet.

I will never forget the pain and helplessness I felt, shortly after we parted, standing by and watching her backslide emotionally, while not being able to do anything to help relieve her pain.

LOCKING IN MY BELIEF IN EVERYDAY MIRACLES

Mom's health was declining. On March 21, 2007, the first day of spring, she passed away. I had seen to it that she was comfortable, loved, and well taken care of in the series of assisted-living facilities that my brother and I had placed her in during the last days of her life.

In February of 2007, it was clear that she was ready to die. I wouldn't realize how ready she was until some time after her death.

We put her in hospice care in Danville, California, a few days before her death. The day before she died, I visited her. A few minutes after I entered her room, she slowly turned her head and smiled gently at me. She seemed far away emotionally, but very much at peace. She also had been holding her spindly little arms straight up in the air when I walked into the room.

I asked the caregiver how long she had been doing this. She said she just started doing it that day. I reached up and gently tried to put her arms down by her side. She resisted with a strength that belied the size of her little arms.

I didn't think much more of it. I kissed her and told her goodbye and that I'd see her tomorrow. I drove back home.

The following morning at 4:00 AM I got a call from the hospice caregiver. She told me that Mom died about a half hour earlier. I jumped in the car and raced to the East Bay from my home in Novato. I wiped away the tears as I drove through the early-morning darkness, cursing myself for not staying with her the last night she was alive.

I walked in, and I reached over and kissed her cold forehead. Her mouth was open and was drooped to the left. I was able to spend an hour or so alone with her, reliving the importance of her in my life, before the morticians arrived.

I watched as the morticians carefully rolled her over and began wrapping her body in a beautiful purple velvet blanket.

I asked if I could help, and they said, "Of course."

I did what I could, being careful not to get in their way. When I saw the hospice lady come into the room, I asked her if Mom had continued to hold her arms in the air after I left the day before. She said, "Yes, your mother held her arms in the air for quite some time after you left."

It was then that I realized that Mom, a faithful Catholic all her life and the woman whom I inherited my love for God from, was extending her arms to her Lord who was welcoming her home. That's all I can figure.

PROOF OF MOM'S MIRACLE

It was five months later, August 2007. I was attending a Catholic men's rite of passage in northern Minnesota for the purposes of comparing this Christian men's initiation with the power of the secular New Warrior Training Adventure that I had led for so many years.

I wanted to see if there would be some indication that this might be a new path for me, where I could bring God into men's lives in conjunction with my former experience in the New Warrior organization.

Another intention was to pray that I would be given a message or a sign that Mom was home and at peace in heaven.

I was still haunted by the sight of her skinny little arms reaching skyward the day before she died. I needed to know if this was just some predeath anomaly or if she was actually seeing beyond the veil and into heaven.

I knew this weekend training included a day of fasting and self-reflection in the woods surrounding the camp where the training was being held. This would be an ideal way to be silent and communicate with God for a sign that Mom was home.

I was afraid that this might be too much to ask of God. I couldn't have been more wrong.

"WHY ARE YOU AFRAID, OH YE OF LITTLE FAITH..."

After our morning gathering and prayer, all of the men who had fasted the night before started to fan out in the surrounding forest in search of a sacred spot.

After passing up a few sites, I found a sweet little clearing just off one of the dirt paths leading through the woods. I spread out my altar cloth and placed a picture of Mom, face up, on the cloth.

Then I leaned back against the tree that would be my backrest for the next eight hours. I consciously opened my heart and my mind to what God had in store for me.

An hour passed, then two. I was afraid that nothing was going to happen, when, out of the corner of my eye, I saw this beautiful, little, orange butterfly fluttering above my head.

She fluttered around and slowly descended toward where I was sitting. It seemed like she was checking out her landing zone to see if it was safe. Then she gently landed right on top of Mom's picture.

I couldn't hold back the tears. They started pouring out of my eyes and streamed down my cheeks. I thought for a moment that the little messenger might sense my tears and be disturbed by them.

The butterfly sat there, atop Mom's picture, for probably ten minutes, fluttering her wings every so often. Then, as silently as she came, she fluttered up and away into the forest.

I sat there in awe at the power of God to have given me that message and in gratitude for the trust that I placed in him to do so, in this most sacred place.

I knew now that Mom was home. I knew that the God that she had so faithfully served had kept his promise and received her. I was grateful that she passed on that gift of faith to me.

A PARTNERSHIP MADE IN HEAVEN

In this book, I often bandy about the terms "miracle" and "blessings." I try not to use those terms lightly. But the only way I could have met and married the most beautiful woman in the world—spiritually, emotionally, physically—after my checkerboard-relationship past was through a series of events and miracles, leading up to our meeting.

This next relationship would be very different.

I attended a Harvest Evangelism conference in Mar del Plata, Argentina, as a participant, helping to transform cities into "marketplace ministries" for God through prayer and intercession in the city population.

As far as I can tell, my wife appeared in my life as a direct result of some two hundred people praying over me and the other single people who had attended the conference.

It was the last night of the conference, and many of us who attended the conference together were eating dinner at a restaurant in the downtown section of Mar del Plata. After dinner, one of the pastors announced that they wanted to pray for all the single people in the audience that God would find the right Godly partner for us.

I remember thinking to myself, *God, I can't believe I came all the way to Argentina, and I'm standing up here on this stage, admitting publicly that I need help to find a wife. But, man, do I ever need this, especially now, at my age, and especially after so many relationship screwups.*

ARGENTINA PRAYERS COME TO FRUITION

Janeth, my wife of the last four years, and I were separated by thirty-eight hundred statute miles, two countries, two different cultures, two mutually unspoken languages, and twenty-three years' difference in age.

We met on a Christian Internet dating site, BigChurch.com. Janeth had logged onto this site for a very short period of time and was not a paying member.

Before we met, I had been talking to a Netjets pilot buddy of mine, complaining about the lack of available, authentic Christian women in Marin County. He told me he was engaged to a beautiful woman from Colombia, and that if I was serious about finding a good woman that I should check out this BigChurch.com dating site where he met his wife-to-be.

I figured, *Hey, I'm striking out regularly in California. Why not? I've got nothing to lose. And I might get lucky.*

It didn't take me long to log onto the website once I arrived at our layover hotel in Cincinnati, Ohio. I typed in the name of the site, went to the Colombia section, and voila, her picture popped up at the top of the list of Colombian women.

She had posted a picture on the site that, while it showed her beauty, by no means reflected the joy, spontaneity, and boundless love that I would come to discover in her.

This woman was far more than I had expected to find on this site. After a closer look, I realized that she was exceedingly beautiful. My heart started to beat so fast I thought it was going to jump out of my chest.

I quickly began to type out an email message to her. Once I finished, I was about to hit the Send button when I thought, *Hey, I bet every*

English-speaking guy in the world is probably hitting on this woman, in English!

Looking back now, what I did then was probably one of the smartest things I have ever done.

I searched the Internet for an English-to-Spanish translation site, popped my email into the translate box, sent it off, and back it came in Spanish.

I copied and pasted it into my email message and sent it off to Colombia. About an hour later, I got a reply from Janeth, in English. She had done the same thing, translated her message in Spanish into English.

Thus began a month-long communication, if you can call it that, between us. I would call her at work in Colombia, on my cell phone, she would answer, and we would chatter away, she in Spanish and I in English, not having a clue what we were saying to each other. We just knew that we didn't need words to express the love that we felt for each other.

This was definitely a match made in heaven. As I thought about the truly miraculous way in which we met, I immediately flashed back to that last night in Mar del Plata, Argentina, some three years prior, when the single men and women were prayed over. Could it be that the prayers brought this woman into my life?

It was especially exciting for me since I had recently been rejected by eHarmony.com. I can only guess that my age, my numerous marriages, and maybe my too-personal and revealing profile turned them off.

Since their success as a dating site depends on positive word-of-mouth advertising, they figured I was a pretty high risk for a successful match up.

After a month of this long-distance "dating," I knew I had to fly to Bogota, Colombia, to meet this woman. In my heart, I knew she was the one I wanted to spend the rest of my life with; but with my past relationship history looming so large in my mind, I wanted to make as sure as I possibly could that this was not just another head fake that I was throwing myself.

And yet I still knew in my heart that this was the woman that I had been waiting so long for. So I took an engagement ring to Bogota with me. When my plane landed and I came out of the Customs area into the terminal where everybody waits for their loved ones, all I saw was this beautiful, little, dark-skinned, dark-haired beauty, jumping up and down, hands waving, shouting at me.

We walked slowly up to one another, looked in each other's eyes, and then we hugged. She tousled her long, black hair, tilted her head back, looked up at the sky, and prayed, "*Gracias por Dios!*" (Thank you for God!)

Instantly, I knew this trip had confirmed what I already knew—that I would spend the rest of my life with this woman. Two days after I arrived in Bogota, I proposed to Janeth, and she accepted. I then wanted to do something I had never done before: ask her father for his daughter's hand in marriage. I figured this was going to be tricky since "Papi" was the same age as me!

It went well, though. I palmed a cheat sheet in my hand with the Spanish words for "I'm asking your permission to marry your daughter" (*Me gustaría su permiso para casarme con su hija*) and referred to it as I made my pitch to him.

I wanted to be sure I wouldn't end up mistakenly asking him something like, "How many bathrooms do you have in the house?"

Over the next year, I would commute to Bogota six times, courting my wife and arranging for the fiancée's visa to bring her into the U.S. for our eventual marriage in July 2009.

THE MIRACLE OF THE NETJETS BUYOUT

Getting hired at Executive Jet was one of the major miracles of my life. That job showed up at the absolute perfect time.

I spent a great nine years there, flying captain on the newest and best equipment that our wealthy clients' money could buy—the Cessna Citation Jet series and Gulfstream G200 aircraft.

During my last few years there, I realized that I would soon leave aviation once again. Not because I couldn't do the job any longer—at age sixty-nine, it felt like I was getting better instead of losing a step as a pilot.

I chose to leave because I was tiring of my thirty-five years of living in hotel rooms and being gone from home half of every month.

But the main reason I wanted to leave was so I could spend as much time as possible with my new wife, helping her to become comfortable in her new country and with her new language and customs. I wasn't going to take any chances with this relationship ending up like all the others, failed because of me not fully being there.

My salary at Netjets, after a long, drawn-out battle between the pilots union and the company, was increased significantly enough so that I was able to rebuild some of the retirement money that I had lost after leaving TWA.

There were also other very important reasons why I had to leave the career that had defined me for most of my life.

Probably the most important factor in my leaving Netjets was another miracle. This one would be a sign that God had something in mind for me that would finally use what He had been grooming me for through all these years of perceived "failures."

I was hired at sixty-one and was now approaching seventy. I knew that even though I had replenished some of my lost TWA retirement money, I didn't have enough to leave Netjets and be able to live comfortably.

During the last few years at Netjets, I would often pray something like, "God, if you have a plan for me besides flying airplanes, then please show me what it is. I know you've given me some gifts and talents that I'm being called to use.

"And I know you've given me the gift of this career for the last thirty-five years, but it feels like my time in the cockpit is over. Please show me how to leave and make clear the transition from this great career into what you're calling me to do.

"Thanks, God. Your son, Bert."

AN ANSWER TO MY PRAYERS

In late 2008, the president and founder of Netjets, Mr. Richard Santulli, made the pilots at Netjets an offer we couldn't refuse. This came about when the company began hemorrhaging massive amounts of dollars as the economy took its toll on the owners' pocketbooks.

Mr. Santulli figured if he could provide enough incentive for the senior pilots to leave the company, then he could possibly avert a pilot furlough.

This was an answer to my prayers.

It took me all of about thirty seconds to put my paperwork in and begin planning my second paid aviation retirement. This buyout would give me three years of a very comfortable salary plus full medical benefits for my new wife and me.

Shortly after the buyout package was announced, Mr. Warren Buffett, the founder and president of Berkshire Hathaway, the parent company of Netjets, went ballistic—I can only imagine since I wasn't there—and fired Mr. Santulli for this most generous but corporately incomprehensible act.

But not before I signed the papers and put my name in the early-retirement hat.

It was announced that Mr. Santulli had "resigned to spend more time with his family," but we all knew that was corporate speak for, "You're fired, dude!" His mistake was being overly generous with the company's money in tough economic times.

Mr. Santulli was the Godfather of Netjets and saw us as his family. Unfortunately, the familial sentiments weren't shared by the higher-ups at Berkshire Hathaway.

There were some anxious moments for those of us pilots who were on critical aircraft fleets, since the buyout would require retraining pilots on other fleets to replace us pilots who were taking the buyout.

But the papers were signed, and, on December 4, 2009, I was officially separated after two of the most miraculous blessings I had ever received: (1) my initial hiring at Netjets when I most needed the money; and (2) the generous offer to leave Netjets after having put in nine of the most enjoyable of my thirty-five years in aviation.

CHAPTER 15

LIVING FROM THE HEART

Early in 2011, I was researching some programs that might combine the best of the powerful New Warrior training I had been part of with some kind of equally powerful Christian-based training.

My research led me to southern California and Bill Berry, a man with a New Warrior background who leads a series of weekend workshops called The Living From the Heart Christian Men's Weekend. Bill is a very skilled, heartfelt facilitator of men's heart-and-soul work, who bridges his background—growing up in the Christian mission fields of South America—with the transformative power of New Warrior training methods.

After I attended three of his trainings over a period of six months or so, I knew this was what I had been looking for. It was time for this work to be brought to the Christian men of Marin County.

In preparation for gathering enough men to conduct a training in Marin, I began leading weekly men's gatherings at my local church, the Novato New Life Christian Center.

Gradually, men trickled to the weekly gatherings, and slowly we collected enough men to make it worthwhile for Bill to travel north to put on his Living From the Heart training at Walker Creek Ranch in Petaluma, California.

Since the completion of that training, one of the most significant parts of my life has been my ongoing weekly meetings with those men who attended that weekend and transformed their lives.

We currently have a group of ten men, and more continue to hear about our group as it grows.

For each of us, our weekly gathering is one of the most important parts of our lives and the highlight of our week. We don't know how we lived without it before.

Not only is this weekly meeting one of my proudest accomplishments, but it also sustains, nurtures, and inspires me to continue to do this kind of work.

The Marin County weekly gathering ranks right up there with my starting the St. Louis New Warrior men's community in 1993. The difference is that this group is somehow more powerful, more sustainable, and more heartfelt because God has His hand in these meetings. The feeling of the Spirit is often palpable in our gatherings.

Before I realized that Beyonce's song "I Was Here" contained the lyrics "Have I lived, have I loved, have I made a difference," these questions seemed to be ever-present in the back of my mind for the past year or so.

As I entered into the final stages of writing and publishing my book over the last year, I reflected more deeply on my life. As I did so, answers to the three questions on the page above have become clear. I hope they provide you with insight also.

HAVE I LIVED?

I have had many adventures; I have been a seeker; I have traveled to many distant, exotic lands; and I have many wonderful memories. I have been told that I have lived a full, interesting, adventurous life, but I have doubts and often feel that I could have done better.

I could have been more conscious in how I chose and treated the women in my life; I could have paid more attention to the management of my money; I could have remained in one place longer and planted roots there. I could have made deeper connections with people and communicated to them their importance in my life more often.

But the presence of the people in my life who love me and exemplify how much I mean to them and how they honor and respect me seems to belie these self-doubts.

If you saw the movie *Saving Private Ryan*, you remember the scene at the end of the movie where an old man and his wife are gathered around the tombstone of the man's fallen friend, Lieutenant John Miller. The old man asks his wife, "Am I a good man?"

He asks this because he was concerned he hadn't lived his life to the fullest, particularly since Lieutenant Miller died saving his life in the war.

If somebody asked you if you have lived your life to the fullest, what would your answer be?

When I asked this question to my men's group, it was met in stony silence.

I spoke up and said, "I'm pretty sure I have." But for you, my reader, ask yourself and contemplate the answer.

I want you to do as I do, to hold those same questions in front of you as you move through your life.

HAVE I LOVED?

My life has been blessed in numerous ways. I was born into a family that loved me. I had a mother who modeled deep faith in God and loved me as unconditionally as any human could. My father was absolutely perfect for teaching me the lessons I needed to learn and that I continue to learn. I grew up in the greatest city in the world, in the most magical, stress-free, abundant time in history. I was an integral part of the mid-'50s hot-rod scene. I was mentored by men who showed up at a time in my life when I needed them, who acted as role models in a way that my pop wasn't capable of. I stumbled into the greatest career possible for a man who loves to be around machines, especially ones that fly. And there's so much more.

But if I had to list the highest and most blessed events of my life that have taught me how to love, I'd mention three: 1) Being by my mother's side as she slipped into dementia from 2004 to 2007, and watching her become increasingly more joyful as her mind seemed to release the stress of worry; 2) Meeting my wife, my ideal woman, four years ago; and 3) Being chased down and nabbed by God in 2004.

In Christian circles, it's customary to list those last two events in reverse order: Loving God is most often listed as the most important priority, and loving family comes next. That's a tough call for me.

Maybe it's because it took me so long to get it right in my relationships, and maybe it's because I got it right so late in life.

But to have met a woman who is so unconditionally loving, so joyful, so filled with the love of God, so authentically gregarious, and such a magnet for others, and to have waited so long to find her, I consider this one of the biggest miracles in my life.

HAVE I MADE A DIFFERENCE?

Yes, I've made a difference. I've made a difference in my life, in the lives of the men whom I've worked with over the years as a leader in the New Warrior Training Adventure, in the lives of the men and women whom I flew with, in the lives of the men and women I've coached, and in the lives of the men whom I meet with weekly as part of our Living From the Heart Christian men's group.

As part of my daily meditative practice, I envision making a difference in the lives of people whom I meet daily by paying attention to them, by looking into the eyes of their hearts, and by speaking joy and laughter into their lives.

I often find myself needing to say, "I don't make as much of a difference as some other people do. But if I allow myself to go into that familiar state of destructive comparison, I have just lost my ability to make a difference!"

If you could take away one thing from my book, I would like for you to apply what you have learned here to your own life.

If you find yourself better equipped to answer, or at least contemplate, these three questions after reading my book, then I have done my job, and you have helped me to have lived, to have loved, and to have made a difference.

I'll see you on the road, in the skies, or on the other side…

RESOURCES

1 Bert's website: http://www.BertBotta.com

My passion and talent is helping to create the kind of strong, accountable, openhearted men that I aspire to become and I want in my life. If you're looking for powerful change in your life and you relate to my story, you will find something here.

Your journey within will provide you with enough adventure, outrageous joy, and fulfillment that will far surpass any item on your "bucket list."

If you choose to do any of the trainings mentioned here, you will return home hungry for how to put what you learned about yourself into action. That's another area where I can help. You can join our group, if you live in the northern California area.

Or we can work together through an individual coaching program that we, you and I, will tailor specifically to your needs.

2 Consulting:

I'm available for consulting to businesses, organizations, and groups who want to achieve more in less time and with greater productivity, passion, and profitability. Interested? Contact me on my website, by phone (415-320-9811), or by email (botajet@mac.com).

3 The Living From the Heart Men's Weekend:
http://www.christianmenswork.com/

I left the ManKind Project as a full, certified leader in 1998. My leaving that work was an unconscious act to find a deeper spiritual connection with God that I didn't find in that community.

During the next ten years, I wondered what God had in mind for me: was I meant to just sit on the sidelines and watch the "walking wounded"—men who live their lives out of that shadowy place that runs and ruins them—continue on that path? Or was I being called to bring what I had learned in the New Warrior community to Christian men, many of whom I judged as "being saved from the neck up."

What I mean by that term is, when I became a Christian, I observed many churchgoing men acting like their spiritual work was complete, having accepted Christ into their hearts while simultaneously sitting on a ton of unresolved anger, rage, powerlessness, self-doubt, criticism, and more.

It was during this phase of my search that I found the Living From the Heart training for Christian men, led by Bill Berry, a gifted facilitator. I attended 3 of Bill's trainings in southern California before I realized that this was what I had been looking for and was being called to create in Marin County, California.

Bill and I made plans to bring this training to Marin County in August of 2011. Since then, 12 men meet weekly in my group in northern California, combining the power of the New Warrior methods of self-inquiry with the healing power of God's Holy Spirit.

Having said all this, it is not mandatory that a man be a Christian to take this training and join this group. Men of all faiths are welcome. The only requirements are an open mind and a willingness to open one's heart and be authentic.

This work is a safe and confidential place to explore the sacred masculine soul that God placed in you. Here you can find practical ways to become the man God created you to be. You can begin to "put on the whole armor of God" (Ephesians 6:11).

This is a very powerful weekend, one that reaches down into the core of your being. At the same time, it is a very safe weekend. It is a time when you can connect to other men in a way seldom experienced in normal church men's retreats and events. Each LFTH Weekend is limited to 16 participants, supported by a staff of 8 experienced men. You will receive personalized attention. You will not get lost in a crowd. All the work you do here is confidential.

4 The ManKind Project®: The New Warrior Training Adventure: http://mankindproject.org

This training was one of the most powerful experiences of my life. I recommend it to any man who wants to live his life at the highest level of integrity, accountability, and authenticity possible. It is not a Christian-based training, but a man comes away from this weekend with a deeper sense of his connection to his own version of spirituality, while simultaneously connecting his head to his heart.

As stated on their website, "The ManKind Project (MKP) is a global nonprofit 501(c)(3) charitable organization that conducts challenging and highly rewarding training for men at every stage of life." They help men through any transition, at all levels of success, and while facing almost any challenge. MKP is not affiliated with any religious practice or political party. Men of all color, belief systems, sexual preference, class, age, ability, ethnicity, and nationality are welcome. Much of the power of this work lies in the follow-up integration groups that meet weekly or biweekly after the weekend training is complete.

5 A Simple System to… Achieve Your Goals and Change Your Life   (eBook coming in 2013)

This is a powerful, simple system to get what you want in your life. If you've tried goal-setting before, forget it! This is much more than that. If you follow the steps of this system, it will take you places you've never been before. And if you're serious, you will get a life that was just a fantasy before.

I think you're going to like this. Read it, then give me a call so I can help you activate it in your life.

6 "God or Money? Can you have both? Learn how a former youth pastor honors God and makes a fortune!"
An interview with Jeff Mills, former Christian youth pastor and now famous, thriving, world-renowned Internet Marketer.

What makes a man successful, and what is his definition of success? What is his humanity like, and how does he walk his talk in everyday life? How does this man, Jeff Mills, embrace traditional Christian values while being successful in the outer world?

I saw a need for interviewing men like Jeff to shine a light on the process of success and what that means to entrepreneurs everywhere. But I'm mainly intrigued by how this applies to Christian men whose belief systems about faith and monetary success often clash. But there's something in this interview for everyone, regardless of your faith or beliefs.

Learn how this Christian businessman embraces and integrates spirituality and success and how the principles in this interview apply to your life.

You can go to my website (http://www.BertBotta.com) and download the interview with Jeff Mills for FREE.

7 Navy SEAL Guts for Christian Men: Facing and Conquering the Enemy Within

This is an eBook based on my interview with Steve Watkins, a former Navy SEAL. The book is available on Amazon.com or on my website: http://www.BertBotta.com.

Steve became a Navy SEAL in 1988, went on to become a sniper and a sniper instructor, and served over 5 years on SEAL Team 5. He participated in Operation Desert Storm and taught on SEAL Team 5's training team for over a year in the area of counterterrorist operations.

In 1996 he attended Master Seminary in Los Angeles and earned a Master of Divinity degree with Honors in May 2000. He's currently teaching religious studies part-time at Northern Kentucky University, and is now a third-year PhD candidate in Humanities at The University of Louisville.

Steve is a Chaplain and a Lieutenant in the US Navy Reserves. He's also an associate pastor in Kentucky and is the author of Meeting God Behind Enemy Lines.

If you're interested in this kind of insight into the power of transformed men and how to take your God-given power and compassion into the world, I'd enjoy talking with you. Call me at 415.320.9811 for a FREE half-hour coaching session, valued at $150.00.

8 Bob Bly, master copywriter and purveyor of valuable, reasonably priced information on just about any subject.

Bob is first of all a copywriter, one of the best. But his talent doesn't stop there. While his website is not directly connected to the theme of my book, I have used Bob's products for the past five years. He is not only one of the most prolific producers of quality content on the internet, but the prices for his products are extremely reasonable for the value they create.

For anyone looking for a "one size fits almost all" place to go and peruse or buy books, eBooks, videos, marketing tools, etc., this is the place. I'm an affiliate of Bob's, and here is the link to his website: http://bit.ly/V3AMyS.

ABOUT THE AUTHOR

Bert Botta was born and raised in San Francisco, California. He was a pilot/instructor for Trans World Airlines for twenty-six years and was in private practice as a professional counselor in St. Louis, Missouri. In 1981, after his third divorce, he began a worldwide spiritual journey.

He returned to TWA, attended the New Warrior Training Adventure in August 1992, and three months later, he took early retirement from his airline. Three years after retiring, he became a certified leader in the New Warrior Training Adventure.

He attended City College of San Francisco, San Francisco State University, and John F. Kennedy University in Orinda, California, where he earned a Master's degree in Counseling Psychology.

After seven years out of the cockpit, he went back to work for Netjets as a captain on Citation and Gulfstream corporate jets.

He envisioned, formed, and co-led the first Living From the Heart Christian Men's training and subsequent community in Marin County, California, in August 2011.